CAMBRIDGE
UNIVERSITY PRESS

T0268553

Chemistry

for Cambridge IGCSE™

PRACTICAL WORKBOOK

Michael Strachan

CAMBRIDGE
UNIVERSITY PRESS

Shaftesbury Road, Cambridge CB2 8EA, United Kingdom

One Liberty Plaza, 20th Floor, New York, NY 10006, USA

477 Williamstown Road, Port Melbourne, VIC 3207, Australia

314–321, 3rd Floor, Plot 3, Splendor Forum, Jasola District Centre, New Delhi – 110025, India

103 Penang Road, #05-06/07, Visioncrest Commercial, Singapore 238467

Cambridge University Press is part of the University of Cambridge.

It furthers the University's mission by disseminating knowledge in the pursuit of education, learning and research at the highest international levels of excellence.

www.cambridge.org
Information on this title: www.cambridge.org/9781108948340

© Cambridge University Press & Assessment 2021

This publication is in copyright. Subject to statutory exception and to the provisions of relevant collective licensing agreements, no reproduction of any part may take place without the written permission of Cambridge University Press.

First published 2016
Second edition 2021

20 19 18 17 16 15 14 13 12 11 10 9 8 7

Printed in the Netherlands by Wilco BV

A catalogue record for this publication is available from the British Library

ISBN 978-1-108-94834-0 Practical Workbook with Digital Access (2 Years)

Additional resources for this publication at www.cambridge.org/go

Illustrations by Tech-Set Ltd

Cambridge International copyright material in this publication is reproduced under licence and remains the intellectual property of Cambridge Assessment International Education.

NOTICE TO TEACHERS IN THE UK

It is illegal to reproduce any part of this work in material form (including photocopying and electronic storage) except under the following circumstances:

(i)   where you are abiding by a licence granted to your school or institution by the Copyright Licensing Agency;

(ii) where no such licence exists, or where you wish to exceed the terms of a licence, and you have gained the written permission of Cambridge University Press;

(iii) where you are allowed to reproduce without permission under the provisions of Chapter 3 of the Copyright, Designs and Patents Act 1988, which covers, for example, the reproduction of short passages within certain types of educational anthology and reproduction for the purposes of setting examination questions.

NOTICE TO TEACHERS

The photocopy masters in this publication may be photocopied or distributed [electronically] free of charge for classroom use within the school or institution that purchased the publication. Worksheets and copies of them remain in the copyright of Cambridge University Press, and such copies may not be distributed or used in any way outside the purchasing institution.

Exam-style questions and sample answers have been written by the authors. In examinations, the way marks are awarded may be different. References to assessment and/or assessment preparation are the publisher's interpretation of the syllabus requirements and may not fully reflect the approach of Cambridge Assessment International Education.

DEDICATED TEACHER AWARDS

Teachers play an important part in shaping futures. Our Dedicated Teacher Awards recognise the hard work that teachers put in every day.

Thank you to everyone who nominated this year; we have been inspired and moved by all of your stories. Well done to all of our nominees for your dedication to learning and for inspiring the next generation of thinkers, leaders and innovators.

Congratulations to our incredible winner and finalists!

WINNER

Patricia Abril	Stanley Manaay	Tiffany Cavanagh	Helen Comerford	John Nicko Coyoca	Meera Rangarajan
New Cambridge School, Colombia	Salvacion National High School, Philippines	Trident College Solwezi, Zambia	Lumen Christi Catholic College, Australia	University of San Jose-Recoletos, Philippines	RBK International Academy, India

For more information about our dedicated teachers and their stories, go to
dedicatedteacher.cambridge.org

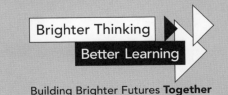

Building Brighter Futures **Together**

> Contents

How to use this series   vi

How to use this book   viii

Introduction   x

Safety   xi

Practical skills and support   xii

1 States of matter

| 1.1 | Changing the physical state of water | 2 |
| 1.2 | Cooling curves | 7 |

2 Atomic structure

| 2.1 | Modelling atomic structure | 13 |
| 2.2 | Calculating the relative atomic mass of an element from the relative masses and abundance of its isotopes | 16 |

3 Chemical bonding

| 3.1 | The differences between elements and compounds | 21 |
| 3.2 | The properties of compounds with ionic and covalent bonding | 24 |

4 Chemical formulae and equations

| 4.1 | Deducing chemical formulae | 32 |
| 4.2 | Reactants and products | 35 |

5 Chemical calculations

5.1	Calculating the ratio of water in hydrated salts	42
5.2	Calculating percentage yield using copper(II) carbonate	46
5.3	Calculating the relative atomic mass of magnesium	50
5.4	Finding the empirical formula of copper oxide	53

6 Electrochemistry

| 6.1 | The electrolysis of copper | 59 |
| 6.2 | Electroplating | 62 |

7 Chemical energetics

| 7.1 | Types of chemical reaction | 70 |
| 7.2 | Endothermic and exothermic reactions | 75 |

8 Rate of reaction

| 8.1 | The effect of temperature on reaction rate | 82 |
| 8.2 | The effect of catalysts on rate of reaction | 87 |

9 Reversible reactions and equilibrium

| 9.1 | Reversible reactions | 93 |
| 9.2 | Making ammonium sulfate – a plant fertiliser | 97 |

10 Redox reactions

| 10.1 | Energy changes during redox reactions | 103 |
| 10.2 | Identifying oxidising and reducing agents | 108 |

11 Acids and bases

11.1	Weak and strong acids	113
11.2	Investigating relative acidity	118
11.3	Investigating relative alkalinity	122
11.4	The pH of oxides	124

12 Preparation of salts

| 12.1 | The preparation of soluble salts | 131 |
| 12.2 | The preparation of insoluble salts | 135 |

13 The Periodic Table

13.1 The properties of Group I
alkali metals   139

13.2 Investigating the properties and trends
of the halogens   142

14 Metallic elements and alloys

14.1 Comparing the general physical
properties of metals and non-metals   147

14.2 The chemical properties of metals   152

15 Reactivity of metals

15.1 Investigating the reactivity series
of metals   158

15.2 Displacement of metals from salts   161

16 Extraction and corrosion of metals

16.1 Producing iron from iron oxide   169

16.2 Producing copper from
copper(II) carbonate   172

16.3 What causes rusting?   174

16.4 Preventing rusting   177

17 Chemistry of the environment

17.1 Estimating the percentage of oxygen
in air   184

17.2 The effects of acid rain on metal   188

17.3 The effect of carbon dioxide on the
atmosphere   192

17.4 Testing the purity of water   196

18 Introduction to organic chemistry

18.1 Testing for saturated and
unsaturated compounds   204

18.2 Chemical reactions of
homologous series   207

19 Reactions of organic compounds

19.1 The manufacture of ethanol by
fermentation   213

19.2 Making esters from alcohols and acids 216

19.3 Cracking hydrocarbons   220

20 Petrochemicals and polymers

20.1 Comparing fuels   226

20.2 Comparing the physical properties
of polymers and the implications
for recycling   230

21 Experimental design and separation techniques

21.1 Filtration, distillation and evaporation 238

21.2 Chromatography   242

22 Chemical analysis

22.1 Using flame tests to identify metals   249

22.2 Identifying anions   252

22.3 Identifying cations   256

22.4 Acid–base titration   260

Glossary   267

Appendix: The Periodic Table   271

> How to use this series

We offer a comprehensive, flexible array of resources for the Cambridge IGCSE™ Chemistry syllabus. We provide targeted support and practice for the specific challenges we've heard that students face: learning science with English as a second language; learners who find the mathematical content within science difficult; and developing practical skills.

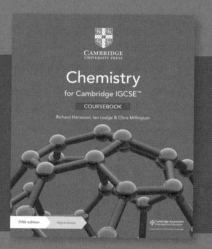

The coursebook provides coverage of the full Cambridge IGCSE Chemistry syllabus. Each chapter explains facts and concepts, and uses relevant real-world examples of scientific principles to bring the subject to life. Together with a focus on practical work and plenty of active learning opportunities, the coursebook prepares learners for all aspects of their scientific study. At the end of each chapter, examination-style questions offer practice opportunities for learners to apply their learning.

The digital teacher's resource contains detailed guidance for all topics of the syllabus, including common misconceptions identifying areas where learners might need extra support, as well as an engaging bank of lesson ideas for each syllabus topic. Differentiation is emphasised with advice for identification of different learner needs and suggestions of appropriate interventions to support and stretch learners. The teacher's resource also contains support for preparing and carrying out all the investigations in the practical workbook, including a set of sample results for when practicals aren't possible.

The teacher's resource also contains scaffolded worksheets and unit tests for each chapter. Answers for all components are accessible to teachers for free on the Cambridge GO platform.

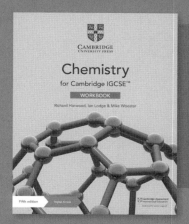

The skills-focused workbook has been carefully constructed to help learners develop the skills that they need as they progress through their Cambridge IGCSE Chemistry course, providing further practice of all the topics in the coursebook. A three-tier, scaffolded approach to skills development enables students to gradually progress through 'focus', 'practice' and 'challenge' exercises, ensuring that every learner is supported. The workbook enables independent learning and is ideal for use in class or as homework.

The practical workbook provides learners with additional opportunities for hands-on practical work, giving them full guidance and support that will help them to develop their investigative skills. These skills include planning investigations, selecting and handling apparatus, creating hypotheses, recording and displaying results, and analysing and evaluating data.

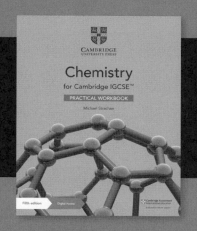

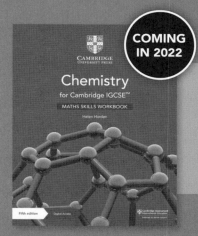

Mathematics is an integral part of scientific study, and one that learners often find a barrier to progression in science. The Maths Skills for Cambridge IGCSE Chemistry write-in workbook has been written in collaboration with the Association for Science Education, with each chapter focusing on several maths skills that students need to succeed in their Chemistry course.

Our research shows that English language skills are the single biggest barrier to students accessing international science. This write-in English language skills workbook contains exercises set within the context of Cambridge IGCSE Chemistry topics to consolidate understanding and embed practice in aspects of language central to the subject. Activities range from practising using the passive form of verbs in the context of electrolysis to the naming of chemical substances using common prefixes.

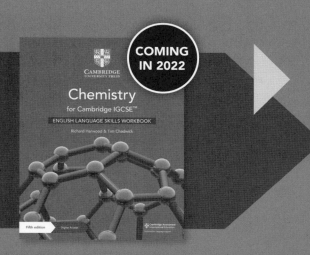

> How to use this book

Throughout this book, you will notice lots of different features that will help your learning. These are explained below.

INTRODUCTION

These set the scene for each chapter and indicate the important concepts. These start with the sentence 'The investigations in this chapter will:'.

KEY WORDS

Key vocabulary and definitions are given at the start of each investigation. You will also find definitions of these words in the Glossary at the back of this book.

Supplement content: In the key word boxes, Supplement content is indicated with a large arrow, as in this example.

COMMAND WORDS

Command words that appear in the syllabus and might be used in exams are highlighted in the exam-style questions. In the margin, you will find the Cambridge International definition. You will also find these definitions in the Glossary at the back of the book.

LEARNING INTENTIONS

These set out the learning intentions for each investigation.

> In the learning intentions table, Supplement content is indicated with a large arrow and a darker background, as in the example here.

The investigations include information on **equipment**, **safety considerations** and **method**. They also include **questions** to test your understanding on recording data, handling data, analysis and evaluation.

Remember that there is a **safety section** at the start of this book – you should refer to this often, as it contains general advice that is applicable to many of the investigations.

REFLECTION

These encourage you to reflect on your learning approaches.

TIPS

The information in these boxes will help you complete the questions, and give you support in areas that you might find difficult.

Supplement content

Where content is intended for students who are studying the Supplement content of the syllabus as well as the Core, this is indicated using the arrow and bar, as on the left here. Some practical investigations that include both Core and Supplement content use this arrow and bar where the main focus of the investigation is on Supplement content.

EXAM-STYLE QUESTIONS

Questions at the end of each chapter provide more demanding exam-style questions, some of which may require use of knowledge from previous chapters. The answers to these questions are accessible to teachers for free on the Cambridge GO site.

Note for teachers:

The teacher's resource in this series includes sample data and support notes for each of the practical investigations in this practical workbook. You can find information about planning and setting up each investigation, further safety guidance, common errors to be aware of, differentiation ideas and additional areas for discussion.

Answers to all questions in this practical workbook are also accessible to teachers at www.cambridge.org/go

> Introduction

None of the pioneering work done in the scientific field of chemistry would ever have occurred without the laboratory and the art of experimentation. Nearly all of the great discoveries that form the foundations of our knowledge came from people completing practical investigations in laboratories not too different from the ones you will be using to complete your studies. Great chemists such as Lavoisier and Priestley, would recognise some of the principles contained in this book, though they would note the modern approaches used to investigate them.

Practical skills form the backbone of any chemistry course and it is hoped that, by using this book, you will gain confidence in this exciting and essential area of study. This book has been written to prepare Cambridge IGCSE™ Chemistry learners for their practical and alternative to practical examinations for Cambridge IGCSE Chemistry (0620/0971). It covers many of the topics from the syllabus. The various investigations and accompanying questions will help you to build and refine your abilities. You will gain enthusiasm in tackling laboratory work and will learn to demonstrate a wide range of practical skills. It is hoped that these interesting and enjoyable investigations will develop in you, a great enthusiasm for practical chemistry. Great care has been taken to ensure that this book contains work that is safe and accessible for you to complete. Before attempting any of these activities, make sure that you have read the safety section and are following the safety regulations of the place where you study. Answers to the exercises in this practical workbook can be found in the teacher's resource. Ask your teacher to provide access to the answers.

> Safety

Despite using Bunsen burners and chemicals on a regular basis, the science laboratory is one of the safest classrooms in a school. This is due to the emphasis on safety and the following of precautions set out by regular risk assessment and procedures.

It is important that you follow the safety rules set out by your teacher. Your teacher will know the names of materials and the hazards associated with them as part of their risk assessment for performing the investigations. They will share this information with you as part of their safety briefing or demonstration of the investigation.

The safety precautions in each of the investigations of this book are guidance that you should follow to ensure your safety and that of other students around you. You should aim to use the safety rules as further direction to help to prepare for examination when planning your own investigations in the practical and alternative to practical papers.

The following precautions will help to ensure your safety when carrying out most investigations in this practical workbook.

- Be careful with chemicals. Never ingest them and always wash your hands after handling them.
- Wear safety goggles to protect your eyes.
- Tie back hair and any loose items of clothing.
- Tidy away personal belongings to avoid tripping over them.
- Wear gloves and protective clothing as described by the book or your teacher.
- Turn the Bunsen burner to the yellow flame when not in use.
- Observe hazard symbols and chemical information provided with all substances and solutions.

Many of the investigations require some sort of teamwork or group work. It is the responsibility of your group to make sure that you plan how to be safe as diligently as you plan the rest of the investigation.

In Chemistry particular attention should be paid to the types of Bunsen burner flame needed as well as the concentrations and volumes of chemicals used.

Cambridge International uses the following hazard codes:
C corrosive, **MH** moderate hazard, **HH** health hazard, **T** acutely toxic, **F** flammable, **O** oxidising, **N** hazardous to the aquatic environment.

You should try to become familiar with these codes.

The information in this section is based on the Cambridge IGCSE and IGCSE (9-1) Chemistry syllabuses (0620/0971) for examination from 2023. You should always refer to the appropriate syllabus document for the year of your students' examination to confirm the details and for more information. The syllabus document is available on the Cambridge International website at www.cambridgeinternational.org.

Note to teachers: Guidance on safety has been included for each of the practical investigations in this practical workbook. You should make sure that they do not contravene any school, education authority or government regulations. You and your school are responsible for safety matters.

> Practical skills and support

The 'Experimental skills and investigations' outlined in the Cambridge IGCSE Chemistry syllabus focus on skills and abilities you need to develop to work as a scientist. Each of these aspects has been broken down for you below with a reference to the chapters in this book that cover it. This will enable you to identify where you have practised each skill and also allow you to revise each one before the exam.

Skills grid

Chapter	1	2	3	4	5	6	7	8	9	10	11	12	13	14	15	16	17	18	19	20	21	22
Experimental skills and investigations																						
1.1 demonstrate knowledge of how to select and safely use techniques																						
1.2 demonstrate knowledge of how to select and safely use apparatus and materials																						
1.3 demonstrate knowledge of how to follow a sequence of instructions where appropriate																						
2 plan experiments and investigations																						
3.1 make and record observations																						
3.2 make and record measurements																						
3.3 make and record estimates																						
4.1 interpret experimental observations and data																						
4.2 evaluate experimental observations and data																						
5.1 evaluate methods																						
5.2 suggest possible improvements to methods																						
Additional skills for Chemistry																						
Constructing own table																						
Drawing/analysing a graph																						
Planning an investigation to improve accuracy/reliability/precision																						
Mathematical calculations																						

Apparatus

You will need to be able to identify, use and draw a variety of scientific apparatus.
Complete the table below by adding a diagram and uses for each piece of apparatus.
The first two pieces of apparatus have been completed for you.

Apparatus	Diagram	Uses	Apparatus	Diagram	Uses
timer		Measure time taken for something to happen. Usually measured in seconds.	balance		Measure mass of a substance. Usually measured in grams.
thermometer			measuring cylinder		
beaker			volumetric pipette		
burette			conical flask		

Apparatus	Diagram	Uses	Apparatus	Diagram	Uses
Bunsen burner			tripod		
gas syringe			test-tube / boiling tube		
filter paper			filter funnel		

Measuring values

Being able to take accurate measurements using a variety of different apparatus is an essential skill in chemistry. It is important that you are familiar with the appropriate apparatus and units for the measurement of volume (liquids and gases), time, temperature, mass and length.

Traditional measuring equipment (e.g. a ruler, measuring cylinder or thermometer) uses a scale made up of equally spaced divisions with numbers marked at regular intervals. These numbers usually increase in values of 1, 2, 5 or 10. You read the measurement from the scale. Not all of the points of the scale will be marked, so you will need to work out the value of each graduation. Data values should be read to an accuracy of one half of one of the smallest divisions on the scale. Digital measuring equipment (e.g. an electronic balance, pH meter, digital timer or temperature probe) display the measurement directly on a small screen.

When using measuring cylinders and burettes for measuring the volume of a liquid you will need to look for the meniscus, which is the bottom of the curved surface formed by the liquid. Always read the measurement from the bottom of the meniscus at eye level. For example, the volume of liquid in the measuring cylinder in Figure P1 is 36.5 cm³.

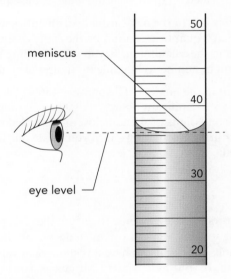

Figure P1: Reading the volume of a liquid.

Recording data

The ability to record data accurately is very important when performing an investigation. Sometimes a table will be supplied for the results; however, you will often need to be able to draw your own table with the correct headings and units.

The first task is to identify the independent and dependent variables for the investigation you are performing. The independent variable is the variable that you are changing to see if this affects the dependent variable. The dependent variable is the variable that you will measure and record the results of in the table. The names of these two variables and their appropriate units need to go into the top two boxes in the columns in your results table. The independent variable goes in the left-hand box and the dependent variable goes in the right-hand box. Separate the name of the variables and units using a forward slash, e.g. volume of gas produced / cm³. Remember that the column headings need to be physical quantities (time, mass, temperature, etc.).

Next, count how many different values you have for the independent variable. This is how many rows you will need to add below the column headings. Finally, add the values for the independent variable into the left-hand column. Your table is now ready for you to add the results from your investigation into the right-hand column. Units are not included with the data in the body of the table.

Independent variable / units	Dependent variable / units

You may need to add extra columns for repeat readings of the dependent variable so that you can calculate a mean (average) value.

The number of decimal places you record in your data will depend on the apparatus used. Data should be recorded to the smallest difference that can be detected on the measuring scale of the equipment.

The number of significant figures should be appropriate to the measuring instrument used. The number of significant figures given for calculated quantities should be the same as the least number of significant figures in the raw data used in the calculation. If you are recording raw data from an investigation, always try to use the maximum number of significant figures available.

The first significant figure is the first non-zero digit in the number. The number 456 is: 500 to 1 significant figure; 460 to 2 significant figures; 456 to 3 significant figures; 456.0 to 4 significant figures, etc. Digits of 5 or greater are rounded up; and digits of 4 and below are rounded down. It is important that numbers are not rounded up during calculations until you have your final answer, otherwise the final answer may be affected.

Drawing graphs

When drawing a graph it is useful to follow a set procedure every time to ensure that when you are finished, the graph is complete. Before starting to draw a graph you must decide on the type of graph. If your independent variable is continuous (one that can have any numerical value, e.g. temperature) then you will need to use a line graph. If your independent variable is categoric (one that has a name, e.g. colour) or discreet (one that has to have a whole number value, e.g. number of layers of insulation) then you will need to use a bar graph.

The first stage of drawing a graph is to label the axes with your independent and dependent variables. The independent variable is used to label the x-axis (horizontal axis) and the dependent variable is used to label the y-axis (vertical axis). Remember to also add the units for each of the variables. An easy way to do this is to copy the column headings from the table of data you are using to draw the graph.

The second stage of drawing a graph is adding a scale. You must select a scale that allows you to use more than half of the graph grid in both directions. Choose a sensible scale to enable you to easily plot your data points, e.g. each 1 cm on the graph grid represents 1, 2, 5 or a multiple of 10 of these numbers (10, 20, 50 or 0.1, 0.2, 0.5). If you choose to use other numbers for your scale it becomes much more difficult to plot your graph.

Now you are ready to plot the points of data on the graph grid. You can use either a cross (×) or a point enclosed inside a circle (⊙) to plot your points, but take your time to make sure these are plotted accurately. Each data point should be plotted to an accuracy of one half of one of the smallest squares on the grid. Remember to use a sharp pencil as large dots make it difficult to see the place the point is plotted.

Finally, a best-fit line needs to be added. This must be a single, thin straight line or smooth curve. It does not need to go through all of the points but it should have roughly half the number of points on each side of the line or curve. Remember to ignore any anomalous data when you draw your best-fit line. Some good examples of straight and curved lines of best fit are shown in Figure P2.

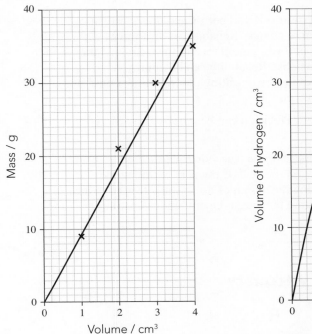 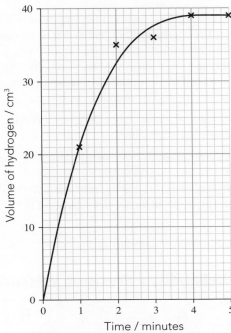

Figure P2 a: Straight line of best fit. **b:** Curved line of best fit.

TIP

Use a transparent ruler when drawing a straight line of best fit. This will allow you see the relative position of all of the data points before you draw the line.

Variables

The independent and dependent variables have already been discussed but there is a third type of variable that you will need to be familiar with – controlled variables. These are variables that are kept the same during an investigation to make sure that they do not affect the results. If these variables are not kept the same then we cannot be sure that it is our independent variable that is having an effect on the results. An investigation where only the independent variable has been allowed to affect the dependent variable is called a 'fair test'.

For example, two students are investigating how changing the temperature affects the rate that gas is produced when adding magnesium to an acid. They do not control the volume of acid or the mass of magnesium used each time. This means that there is no pattern in their results, because if they use more acid or magnesium, more gas is produced regardless of the temperature used. Their investigation is not a fair test.

Reliability, accuracy and precision

A common task is to suggest how to improve the method used in an investigation to improve its reliability/accuracy/precision. It is important that you have a solid understanding of what each of these words mean.

- Reliability refers to the likelihood of getting the same results if you performed the investigation again and being sure that the results are not just down to chance. Reliability is also often called repeatability for this reason. If you can repeat an investigation several times and get the same result each time, the investigation is said to be reliable. Reliability can be improved by controlling other variables so they do not affect the results, by repeating the experiment until no anomalous results are achieved, and by increasing precision.

- Precision indicates the spread of results from the mean. Precision can be improved by using apparatus that has smaller scale divisions.

- Accuracy is a measure of how close the measured value is to the true value. The accuracy of the results depends on the measuring apparatus used and the skill of the person taking the measurements. Accuracy can be improved by improving the design of an investigation to reduce errors, by using more precise apparatus, and by repeating the measurement and calculating the mean.

You can see how these terms are used in Figure P3.

Reliability v Precision v Accuracy

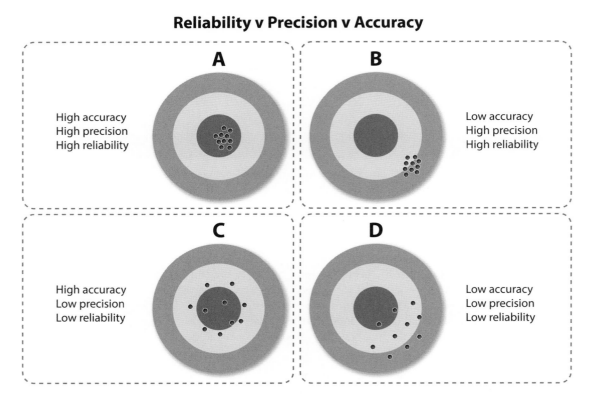

A
High accuracy
High precision
High reliability

B
Low accuracy
High precision
High reliability

C
High accuracy
Low precision
Low reliability

D
Low accuracy
Low precision
Low reliability

Figure P3: Reliability versus precision versus accuracy.

Almost every measurement has some degree of error or uncertainty in it. Identifying sources of error is also important when evaluating experimental methods and suggesting possible improvements.

- Measurement errors result in a difference between a measured value and the true value. Measurement errors can be reduced by taking more careful readings.

- Random errors are unpredictable errors that cause results to vary from one measurement to the next. Random errors can be reduced by taking repeated readings and calculating a mean value.

- Systematic errors cause readings to differ from the true value by the same amount each time a measurement is taken. Systematic errors can be removed by using different apparatus or improved technique. A zero error is a type of systematic error that occurs when a measuring device gives a reading when the true value should be zero (e.g. if a balance shows '4 g' when nothing is on the balance, then all readings from the balance will be 4 g higher than the true values).

An anomalous measurement does not fit the expected trend. This may be due to measurement error or a problem with the equipment. Anomalous measurements should be ignored if it is not possible to repeat the measurement.

Designing an investigation

When asked to design an investigation you must think carefully about what level of detail to include. You must identify what your independent variable is and which values you are planning to use for it. The dependent variable must also be identified along with how you are going to measure it. You will also need to suggest how you will control other variables.

The next step is to suggest the most appropriate apparatus and techniques. The experimental procedure should be outlined in a series of numbered steps that is detailed enough for someone else to follow the method. You should also identify risks and describe any safety precautions.

Finally, you should show how to record and process the results of the investigation. Remember to include repeat readings to help improve reliability and be aware of possible sources of errors.

It is also important that you are familiar with the background chemistry as this will enable you to evaluate the data and form conclusions from the investigation.

> ## Chapter 1
States of matter

THE INVESTIGATIONS IN THIS CHAPTER WILL:

- develop your knowledge of three states of matter: solid, liquid and gas

- focus on the changes between each state

- show you that by changing the temperature of a substance, you can change the state that it exists in

> enable you to explain that when changing states, energy is needed to break the intermolecular forces between molecules.

Practical investigation 1.1: Changing the physical state of water

KEY WORDS

boiling point: the temperature at which a liquid boils, when the pressure of the gas created above the liquid equals atmospheric pressure

freezing point: the temperature at which a liquid turns into a solid – it has the same value as the melting point; a pure substance has a sharp freezing point

intermolecular forces: the weak attractive forces which act between molecules

matter: anything that occupies space and has mass

melting point (m.p): the temperature at which a solid turns into a liquid – it has the same value as the freezing point; a pure substance has a sharp melting point

IN THIS INVESTIGATION YOU WILL:

- examine changes of state in terms of melting, boiling and freezing

- learn how to use a Bunsen burner safely

- draw a graph to show trends in the data.

YOU WILL NEED:

- clamp stand with clamp and boss   • heat-resistant mat   • ice   • timer
- Bunsen burner   • thermometer   • beaker (250 cm³)   • pestle   • mortar   • tripod
- gauze   • stirring rod   • safety glasses   • lab coat   • gloves.

Safety

- Wear eye protection throughout.
- As you will be using hot liquids, you will need to stand for the practical.
- Remember to take care when handling hot glassware and be careful when the water is boiling as the steam will be very hot.

Getting started

Think about how ice keeps a drink cold even on a very hot day. Why does the drink not get warm until all the ice has melted?

....

You will be using a Bunsen burner in this experiment. To be successful you will need to be able to change the type of flame produced by the burner. This is done by adjusting the small collar at the base of the burner to make the vent hole larger or smaller. When the collar is adjusted so that the vent is closed, a yellow flame is produced. This is the lowest temperature flame. If the vent is halfway open, a gentle blue flame is produced. When the vent is fully open, a roaring blue flame is produced. This is the hottest temperature flame. It is important to use the correct flame to get the appropriate temperature.

Method

1   Add seven ice cubes to the mortar and crush them with the pestle until you are left with only small pieces. Do this carefully so that the ice cubes do not escape from the mortar.

> **TIP**
>
> If you have large ice cubes, it might be best to crush the cubes one at a time.

2   Place the crushed ice in the beaker until the beaker is half full.

3   Set up the Bunsen burner on the heat-resistant mat.

4   Place the beaker on the tripod and gauze. Use the clamp and clamp stand to hold the thermometer in the beaker. You can use the diagram in Figure 1.1 to help you.

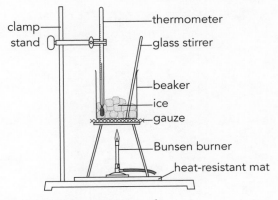

Figure 1.1: Setup for measuring the changing state of ice.

5 Measure the temperature of the ice in the beaker. Record the result in the results table in the Recording data section.

6 Start the timer. Begin to heat the beaker of water with the Bunsen burner on a gentle blue flame.

7 Record the temperature every minute. Use the stirring rod to make sure the ice melts evenly. Once the water is boiling (you can see bubbles forming within the liquid), only take one more reading.

Recording data

1 Record your results in the table provided. The units are missing and need to be added.

Time /.....	0	1	2	3	4	5	6	7	8
Temperature /.....									

Handling data

2 Construct a graph to show the results of your experiment. Think about whether you will need to plot a line graph or a bar graph.

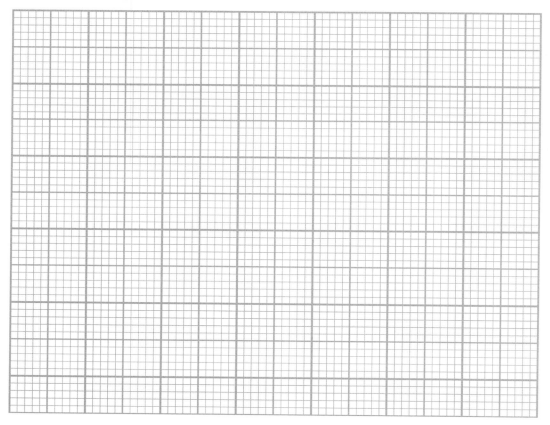

> **TIP**
>
> Use a sharp pencil and a ruler to draw your graph.
>
> Points on the graph should be clearly marked as crosses (×) or encircled dots (☉).

Analysis

3   Use the words below to complete the conclusions.

> **boiling   gas   heating   intermolecular**
>
> **liquid   melting   molecules   temperature**

At first the .... inside the beaker did not change. This is because the energy

being added by .... was being used to break the .... forces

between the water .... in the solid state. This is called ....

Once all the solid water had turned into .... water, the temperature began to

increase. The temperature stopped increasing once the water reached its ....

point. The energy being added was now used to break the intermolecular forces between

the water molecules in the liquid state. This meant that the water could turn into

a ....

4   Look at the graph in Figure 1.2.

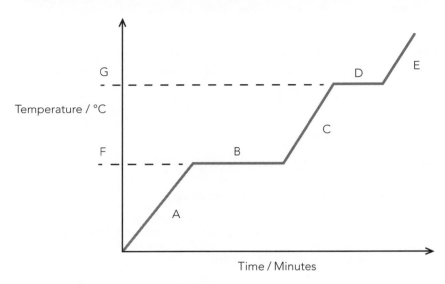

Figure 1.2: A graph to show the heating of a substance.

Match the correct letter to each of the following words or terms:

a   Melting point: ....   d   Liquid: ....

b   Boiling point: ....   e   Gas: ....

c   Solid: ....

Evaluation

5   Think about your experiment. How could you have made the results more accurate?

....

....

....

....

6   You could add an impurity, such as salt, to the ice in this experiment.
     Suggest how this impurity would affect the results. Sketch a graph to support your ideas.

....

....

....

....

REFLECTION

Practical experiments are an important part of chemistry. Think about how you performed this practical.

Were you confident handling the apparatus?

Were you able to use your background knowledge of the subject to help you in the analysis and evaluation?

Practical investigation 1.2: Cooling curves

IN THIS INVESTIGATION YOU WILL:

- examine the effect of temperature on the movement of particles in liquids and solids

- construct a cooling curve from the data you obtain

- interpret a cooling curve.

YOU WILL NEED:

- clamp stand with two clamps and bosses   • heat-resistant mat
- Bunsen burner   • thermometer   • beaker (250 cm^3)   • timer   • tripod   • gauze
- boiling tube containing stearic acid   • safety glasses   • lab coat   • gloves.

Safety

- Wear eye protection throughout.
- As you will be using hot liquids, you will need to stand for the practical.
- Remember to take care when handling hot glassware and also to be careful when the water is boiling as the steam will be very hot.

Getting started

As substances cool, they can change from one state into another state. What do you think will happen to the temperature recorded during these changes of state?

....

You will be using a thermometer in this investigation. Make sure you know how to use the thermometer to accurately measure temperature.

See the Practical skills and support section at the start of this workbook for more information about how to take reliable readings with a thermometer.

Method

1   Set up the Bunsen burner on the heat-resistant mat. Place the tripod over the Bunsen burner and add the gauze to the tripod.

2   Measure 150 cm³ of water and add the water to the beaker. Place the beaker onto the gauze.

3   Fix the clamps and bosses to your clamp stand and place the apparatus next to your tripod.

4   Clamp the boiling tube with the stearic acid so that the boiling tube is held in the beaker of water. See Figure 1.3 for guidance.

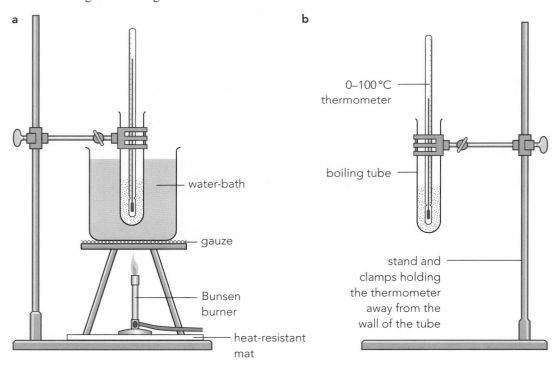

Figure 1.3 a: Heating the stearic acid in a water-bath. **b:** Cooling the stearic acid.

5   Light the Bunsen burner and heat the beaker of water on a gentle blue flame. Heat the water so that it is just boiling gently. You will need to move the Bunsen burner from under the tripod to achieve a gentle boil.

6   As the stearic acid melts, add the thermometer to the boiling tube. Use a clamp to hold the thermometer away from the wall of the boiling tube (Figure 1.3a). Once the thermometer reads 75 °C turn off the Bunsen burner and lift the clamp so that the boiling tube is out of the water (Figure 1.3b).

7   You will need to design your data collection table in the Recording data section. Then record the temperature and start the timer. Record the temperature every 30 seconds until the temperature reaches 45 °C. Do not remove the thermometer from the boiling tube or attempt to stir the stearic acid, as the thermometer might break.

Recording data

1   Design a results table for your investigation in the space provided. You do not yet know how many readings you will need to take. Think about this when you are drawing your table.

Handling data

2   Construct a graph to show the results of your experiment. Think about whether you will need to plot a line graph or a bar graph.

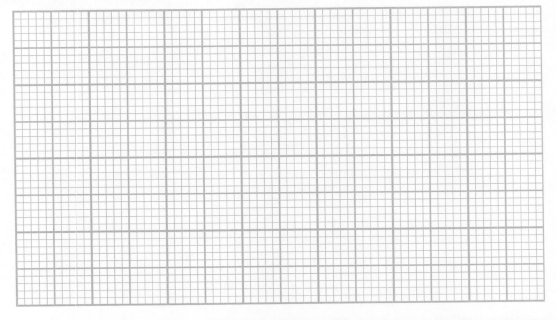

3   Add a curve of best fit to the graph to show the temperature change. You will need to draw the curve freehand without using a ruler.

⟩ Analysis

4   The graph you have drawn is known as a cooling curve. Look at your graph to help you complete the following sentences.

The substance cooled from a temperature of ....°C to a temperature of

...................°C in .... minutes.

The freezing point was ....°C.

5   How long did it take for your sample to freeze?

....

Evaluation

6   Describe how you could improve the method to get more accurate readings for the temperature.

....

....

....

7   Why was the stearic acid heated in a water-bath and not heated directly with a Bunsen flame?

....

....

8   Stearic acid is a waxy solid found in various animal and plant fats. Suggest why stearic acid was used instead of water for this investigation.

....

....

9   How could you make the experiment safer? Suggest one improvement.

....

....

EXAM-STYLE QUESTIONS

1   Two students were investigating how a new type of antifreeze affects the boiling point of water.

   a   Use the thermometer diagrams in each table to complete the results column for the boiling point temperature.

Mass of antifreeze added / g	Thermometer diagram	Boiling point / °C	Mass of antifreeze added / g	Thermometer diagram	Boiling point / °C
0	105 100 95		60	100 95 90	
20	100 95 90		80	85 80 75	
40	95 90 85		100	80 75 70	

[6]

   b   Plot the points on the grid and draw a smooth line graph.

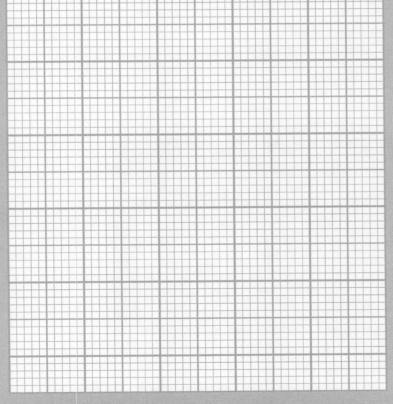

[6]

CONTINUED

c **Consider** which of your results is an anomaly.

....

.... [1]

d Use your graph to find the boiling point of water with 90 g of antifreeze dissolved in it.

.... [1]

e **Suggest** one control variable for this experiment.

....

.... [1]

[Total: 15]

COMMAND WORDS

consider: review and respond to given information

suggest: apply knowledge and understanding to situations where there are a range of valid responses in order to make proposals / put forward considerations

2 Two students are investigating changes of state by heating ice cubes in a beaker using a Bunsen burner. They are recording the temperature of the contents of the beaker every minute. The students suggest four improvements to the method that they think will make their experiment more reliable.

a Read the student's four suggestions.

Tick the box if you think the suggestion will make the experiment more reliable.

Use a silver tripod instead of a black tripod. ☐

Repeat the experiment and calculate a mean temperature for melting and boiling point. ☐

Weigh the mass of ice used. ☐

Use a machine to stir the water, instead of stirring the water by hand. ☐

[2]

b Find an example of where adding an impurity to water to change its melting or boiling point is used in everyday life. **Explain** why the melting point or boiling point is changed, with reference to the intermolecular forces between water molecules.

....

....

....

.... [2]

[Total: 4]

Chapter 2

Atomic structure

THE INVESTIGATIONS IN THIS CHAPTER WILL:

- develop your understanding of how atoms are made of small particles
- show you that different subatomic particles have different properties
- enable you to understand the concept of electron orbitals or shells

> explore how the masses and abundance of isotopes are used to calculate the relative atomic mass of elements.

Practical investigation 2.1: Modelling atomic structure

KEY WORDS

electron: a subatomic particle with negligible mass and a charge of −1; electrons are present in all atoms, located in the shells (energy levels) outside the nucleus

electron shells (energy levels): (of electrons) the allowed energies of electrons in atoms – electrons fill these shells (or levels) starting with the one closest to the nucleus

mass number (or nucleon number) (A): the total number of protons and neutrons in the nucleus of an atom

neutron: an uncharged subatomic particle present in the nuclei of atoms – a neutron has a mass of 1 relative to a proton

proton: a subatomic particle with a relative mass of 1 and a charge of +1 found in the nucleus of all atoms

proton number (or atomic number) (Z): the number of protons in the nucleus of an atom (see also **atomic number**)

subatomic particles: very small particles – protons, neutrons and electrons – from which all atoms are made

IN THIS INVESTIGATION YOU WILL:

- learn where protons, neutrons and electrons are located in the nucleus
- create a model to show the structure of an atom
- calculate the mass number of an element.

YOU WILL NEED:

- small multi-coloured sweets/candies or plastic discs (20 of each of three different colours) • Periodic Table • blank Bohr model templates • lab coat • gloves.

Getting started

Discuss with your partner why it is a good idea to make a model to show the structure of an atom.

Decide which colour of sweet/disc you will use to represent each subatomic particle.

Note: the term subatomic particles, while a useful description, is not an essential term to learn.

	Particle		
	Proton	Neutron	Electron
Colour			

Method

1   Collect 20 of each of the three colours of sweet/disc that you have chosen (total of 60 sweets/discs). Collect your Bohr model template. Place the template in the middle of your desk.

TIP

Due to the nature of this task you must work carefully. The sweets could be moved easily if care is not taken to avoid knocking the workbench or desk.

2   Look at the Periodic Table. Identify the number of protons in lithium. Using the colour of sweets/discs you have chosen for protons, place the same number of sweets in the nucleus on the template.

3   Look at the Periodic Table. Identify the mass number of lithium. Calculate the number of neutrons in lithium by subtracting the number of protons from the mass number.

4   Using the colour of sweets/discs you have chosen for neutrons, place the same number of sweets in the nucleus on the template.

5   Check that the total number of sweets/discs in the nucleus is equal to the mass number of lithium.

6   The number of electrons is the same as the number of protons. Using the colour of sweets/discs you have chosen for electrons, place the same number of sweets in the correct electron shells around the nucleus on the template.

TIP

There are rules for the number of electrons that can fit into each electron shell. The first shell has a maximum of two electrons. The second shell has a maximum of eight electrons. The third shell has a maximum of eight electrons.

7   Repeat steps 2–6 with four other elements from the first 20 elements on the Periodic Table.

See Chapter 2 in the Coursebook for more information about Bohr's theory of the arrangement of electrons in an atom.

TIP

The Bohr model is one way that scientists show the structure of an atom. You do not need to know about Bohr or the name of this model.

Recording data

1   Complete the table below to record how many subatomic particles were used for each element.

Element	Proton number	Number of protons	Number of neutrons	Number of electrons	Mass number
Lithium					

Analysis

2   State the general trend for the mass number as the proton number increases.

....

3   Based on the pattern in your results table, use the following words to complete the sentences below (not all of the words are used).

decreases   equal   increases   same

The numbers of protons and electrons are always the ....

The mass number is the .... as the number of protons added to the number of neutrons.

The numbers of protons and neutrons are not always ....

As the proton number increases, the mass number ....

Evaluation

4   Suggest two ways the model used is an accurate representation of the Bohr model of atomic structure.

....

....

5   Suggest two ways the model used is not an accurate representation of the Bohr model of atomic structure.

....

....

REFLECTION

You have used a model to show the structure of an atom. Think about what you have learnt about models. Does using models help you to understand different concepts and ideas?

What do you think are the limitations of using models?

....

....

Practical investigation 2.2: Calculating the relative atomic mass of an element from the relative masses and abundance of its isotopes

KEY WORD

isotopes: atoms of the same element that have the same proton number but a different nucleon number; they have different numbers of neutrons in their nuclei; some isotopes are radioactive because their nuclei are unstable (radioisotopes)

IN THIS INVESTIGATION YOU WILL:

- learn that elements can exist as different isotopes

  > calculate the relative atomic mass (A_r) of an element using isotope data

- use models to obtain data.

YOU WILL NEED:

- isotope cards • Periodic Table.

Getting started

Look at the Periodic Table in the Appendix.

Find an element that does not have a whole number for its relative atomic mass.

Write the name of this element here: ....

It is not possible for atoms to have half protons or half neutrons. How is it possible for an element to have a relative atomic mass that is not a whole number?

....

....

Method

1   Collect a Periodic Table and have it visible on your desk.

2   Collect a set of isotope cards for an element.

3   Carefully count the number of protons and neutrons for each isotope of the element.

4   Record the data in the results table in the Recording data section.

TIP
You will be counting large numbers of protons and neutrons. A tally chart might be useful.

5   Look at the card for each isotope and record the abundance of each isotope in the results table.

6   Repeat steps 2–5 with the next element.

Recording data

1   Record your data in the results table.

Element	Isotope 1		Isotope 2		Isotope 3	
	Mass	Abundance	Mass	Abundance	Mass	Abundance
Carbon	....	....	....	....	....	....
	Mass	Abundance	Mass	Abundance		
Chlorine	....	....	....	....		

Element	Isotope 1		Isotope 2		Isotope 3	
Copper	Mass	Abundance	Mass	Abundance		
Bromine	Mass	Abundance	Mass	Abundance		

Handling data

To calculate the relative atomic mass of each element, the mass and abundance of each isotope must be used.

The formula for calculating the relative atomic mass of an element is:

$$\text{relative atomic mass} = \frac{\text{total mass of 100 atoms}}{100}$$

For example:

Silver has two isotopes:

Element	Isotope 1		Isotope 2	
	Mass	Abundance	Mass	Abundance
Silver	107	51.4%	109	48.6%

$$\text{relative atomic mass of silver} = \frac{(51.4 \times 107) + (48.6 \times 109)}{100} = 108$$

2   Calculate the relative atomic mass for each of the elements you have investigated. Record values to one decimal place.

$$\text{relative atomic mass of carbon} = \frac{(\quad \times \quad) + (\quad \times \quad) + (\quad \times \quad)}{100} = \text{..........}$$

$$\text{relative atomic mass of chlorine} = \frac{(\quad \times \quad) + (\quad \times \quad)}{100} = \text{..........}$$

relative atomic mass of copper =

relative atomic mass of bromine =

Analysis

Compare your calculation for the relative atomic mass of each element to the value in the Periodic Table.

3 Fill in the table below with your data and the data from the Periodic Table. Give your answers to one decimal place.

Element	Relative atomic mass from calculations	Relative atomic mass from the Periodic Table	Difference = calculated value – Periodic Table value
Carbon			
Chlorine			
Copper			
Bromine			

4 Were any of your calculated values different from the Periodic Table values?

....

Evaluation

5 Think about the method for this investigation. Suggest possible sources of error.

....

....

6 How could you have obtained more reliable data for this investigation?

....

....

7 In the Analysis section you compared your results with the values used on the Periodic Table. Why do scientists need to check their data with known reference values?

....

....

....

EXAM-STYLE QUESTIONS

1 Two students are trying to make a model of an atom. They have different pieces of fruit. The fruit they have are apples, oranges and grapes.

   a The students decide to use the apples to show the protons in an atom.

     i Which fruit should they use to show the neutrons?

.... [1]

ii **Give** a reason for your answer.

.... [1]

iii Which fruit could be used to show the electrons?

.... [1]

iv **Give** a reason for your answer.

.... [1]

b One student draws a circle on a piece of paper. She places five apples inside the circle to show that the element she is modelling has five protons. **State** which element this proton number represents.

.... [1]

[Total: 5]

COMMAND WORDS

give: produce an answer from a given source or recall/memory

state: express in clear terms

2 A student is attempting to calculate the relative atomic mass (A_r) of an unknown element Q. He has the data below on the number of protons and neutrons in each of the two isotopes.

a **Calculate** the mass number for each of the isotopes and add your answers to complete the table.

Isotope of Q	Isotope 1	Isotope 2
Number of protons	44	44
Number of electrons	45	46
Mass number	....	....

[2]

The abundance for each isotope is:
Element Q isotope 1 abundance = 55%
Element Q isotope 2 abundance = 45%

b Using the data for the mass number for each isotope calculated in part **a** and the abundance values, **show that** the A_r of element Q is 89.5.

....

....

....

....

....

[3]

[Total: 5]

COMMAND WORDS

calculate: work out from given facts, figures or information

show (that): provide structured evidence that leads to a given result

Chapter 3

Chemical bonding

THE INVESTIGATIONS IN THIS CHAPTER WILL:

- investigate the differences between elements and compounds

- explore the differences between different types of bonding

- focus on how the type of bonding present in different compounds relates to the properties and uses of the compounds.

Practical investigation 3.1: The differences between elements and compounds

KEY WORDS

compound: a substance formed by the chemical combination of two or more elements in fixed proportions

element: a substance which cannot be further divided into simpler substances by chemical methods; all the atoms of an element contain the same number of protons

IN THIS INVESTIGATION YOU WILL:

- identify the properties of elements and compounds

- make observations of changes in physical properties

- draw conclusions based on the data obtained.

YOU WILL NEED:

- ignition tube/test-tube with iron powder and sulfur powder • Bunsen burner
- tongs • heat-resistant mat • bar magnet • safety glasses • lab coat
- sealed test-tube with a mixture of iron and sulfur • gloves.

Safety

- The ignition tube will be prepared for you. Do not remove the mineral wool plug.

- Wear eye protection throughout.

Getting started

You will be using an ignition tube in this investigation. Examine the ignition tube and the mineral wool plug. Why do you think an ignition tube is being used instead of a normal test-tube?

....

....

Method

1   Look at the mixture of iron and sulfur. Record your observations in the table in the Recording data section.

> **TIP**
>
> An observation is something that you can physically experience, e.g. you can see effervescence in a test-tube or hear a squeaky pop for a gas test. A conclusion is the explanation for the observation, e.g. you would see effervescence if a gas was produced or hear a squeaky pop if the gas was hydrogen.

2   Using the bar magnet, test the mixture of iron and sulfur in the test-tube to see if anything happens. You are looking to see if the mixture, or either of the components of the mixture, is affected by the magnet, e.g. is the mixture pulled to the side of the test-tube?
    Record your observations.

3   Set up your Bunsen burner. Do not light the Bunsen burner until your teacher tells you to do so.

4   Place the ignition tube into the tongs.

5   Heat the ignition tube on a blue flame until the mixture begins to glow. Once this happens, remove the ignition tube from the flame and place the tube on the heat-resistant mat.
    Be careful as the tube will be very hot.

6   Turn your Bunsen burner off.

7   Once your ignition tube has cooled, look at the appearance of the contents of the tube.
    Record your observations in the table.

8   Use the bar magnet to test the new compound to see if the compound is magnetic.
    Record your observations in the table.

Recording data

1   Complete the word equation for the reaction: iron + sulfur → ....

> **TIP**
>
> Compounds made of only two elements have the ending *-ide*.

2 Add the name of the compound formed to the table below and complete the table.

Substance	Appearance	Magnetic or non-magnetic?
Iron and sulfur mixture		

Analysis

3 What signs are there that a chemical reaction was taking place?

....

Evaluation

4 Why was there a mineral wool plug in the ignition tube?

....

....

5 Why might there still be some iron and sulfur inside the ignition tube?

....

....

6 Could this experiment be repeated by replacing iron with copper? Give a reason to support your answer.

....

....

....

REFLECTION

How does an observation relate to a conclusion?

How do you think understanding the difference between an observation and a conclusion will help you in your practical work and your overall learning of chemistry?

....

....

Practical investigation 3.2: The properties of compounds with ionic and covalent bonding

KEY WORDS

covalent bonding: chemical bonding formed by the sharing of one or more pairs of electrons between two atoms

ionic bonding: a strong electrostatic force of attraction between oppositely charged ions

IN THIS INVESTIGATION YOU WILL:

- learn about the differences between compounds with ionic bonding and covalent bonding

- describe the key physical features of covalent and ionic substances

- make careful observations from a series of tests

- use physical properties to classify a substance as ionic or covalent.

YOU WILL NEED:

- crucibles • Bunsen burner • heat-resistant mat • clay triangle • tripod
- spatula • beaker (250 cm³) • distilled water • glass rod
- measuring cylinder (100 cm³) • battery pack or 6 V DC power supply
- wires with crocodile clips • 6 V bulb • graphite rods • two-hole rubber stopper
- clamp stand with clamp and boss • Beaker (100 cm³)
- abrasive paper, such as emery paper • samples of wax, sugar, sodium chloride, silicon oxide, magnesium sulfate, zinc chloride • safety glasses • lab coat • gloves.

Safety

- Take care not to touch the graphite electrodes as you will create a short circuit.

- As soon as the zinc chloride sample melts, stop heating the sample otherwise chlorine gas may be produced.

- Wear eye protection throughout.

Getting started

Look at the power supply. Make sure the power supply is unplugged. Practise setting the power supply to different voltages. It is important that you are able to set the power supply to the correct voltage for this investigation.

Method

You can complete the different parts of this investigation in any order.

Melting point

1 Place a small sample of the substance in a crucible.

2 Rest the clay triangle so that it sits securely in the middle of the tripod (Figure 3.1) and place the crucible in the clay triangle.

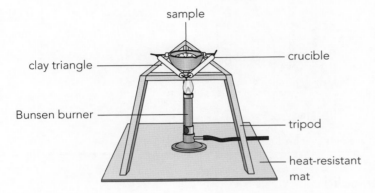

Figure 3.1: Setup showing how to place a clay triangle on a tripod.

3 Heat the sample using the Bunsen burner on a blue flame.

4 Stop heating as soon as the substance begins to melt. If the substance does not melt, try heating the substance with a roaring flame. If the substance still does not melt, record this in your results table. (You will need to design your data collection table in the Recording data section.) Be aware that some samples may spit (bubble or eject small pieces from the sample) when heated.

5 Repeat steps 1–4 with each of the other samples, using a clean crucible each time.

Solubility

1 Add 100 cm³ of water to a beaker. Use a spatula to add a small amount of the substance to the beaker. Stir the mixture with the glass rod. Check if the substance dissolves and record your observations.

2 Repeat step 1 using fresh water for each of the other samples.

Electrical conductivity in solution

1 Set up a simple circuit as shown in Figure 3.2.

2 Half fill a 100 cm³ beaker with water. Add one spatula of the substance to the beaker.

3 Insert the graphite rods (electrodes) into the beaker. Use the two-hole rubber stopper with the clamp and stand to hold the electrodes in place.

4 Turn on the power supply. Check if the bulb lights up and record your observations.

5 Turn off the power supply. Pour away the water and rinse the beaker. Repeat steps 2–4 for each of the other samples.

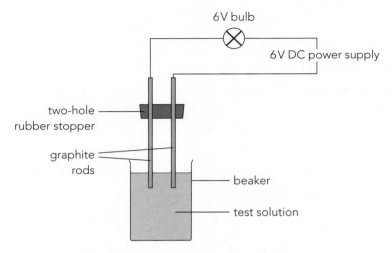

Figure 3.2: Setup to measure the electrical conductivity of a solution.

Electrical conductivity when solid

1 Set up a simple circuit as shown in Figure 3.3.

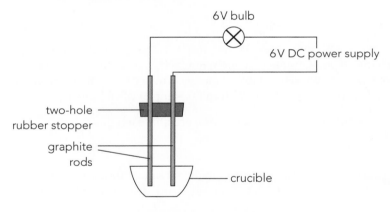

Figure 3.3: Setup to measure electrical conductivity in solids.

2 Use the two-hole rubber stopper with the clamp and stand to hold the electrodes in place.

3 Add three spatulas of the substance being tested, to the crucible.

4 Test the electrical conductivity of the substance by lowering the electrodes into the crucible and turning on the power supply. Make sure the electrodes are not touching. Check if the bulb lights up and record your observations.

5 Turn off the power supply, remove the crucible and then repeat steps 3–4 for each of the different samples.

Electrical conductivity when molten

1   Set up the simple circuit and apparatus as shown in Figure 3.4. Prepare your electrodes, rubber stopper and clamp stand so that the electrodes can be lowered into the crucible easily.

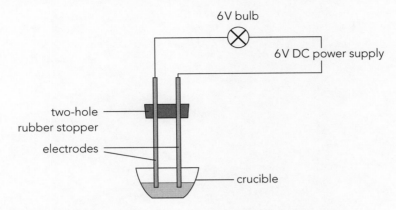

Figure 3.4: Setup to measure electrical conductivity in molten solids.

2   Remove the crucible from the setup and half fill with sugar.

3   Using the setup shown in Figure 3.1, place the crucible in the clay triangle.

4   Heat the crucible gently until the substance just melts. Turn off the Bunsen burner and lower the electrodes into the molten substance. Turn on the power supply. Check if the bulb lights up and record your observations. Take extra care as the molten solid will be very hot.

5   Turn off the power supply and carefully remove the crucible from the clay triangle.

6   Clean the electrodes with the abrasive paper.

7   Repeat steps 2–6 for each of the other samples.

Recording data

1   You will need to design a results table that will include all of the five substances being tested. There are also five different tests being performed. Use the space on the next page to design your table.

Handling data

2   For each of the substances tested, add them to the correct part of the Venn diagram shown.

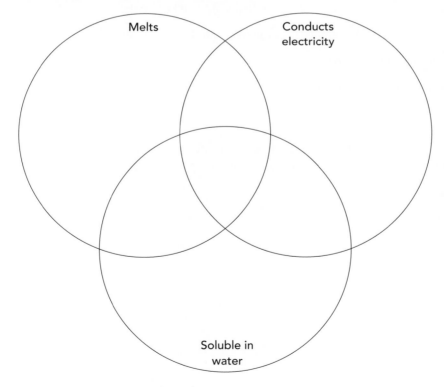

Figure 3.5: A Venn diagram to show physical properties.

> **TIP**
>
> Venn diagrams use overlapping circles to illustrate the relationships between and within different groups.

3   One of the substances does not fit anywhere on the Venn diagram. Which substance is this?

....

Analysis

4   Fill in the table below.

The properties of ionic compounds	Substances tested that had these properties
....	....
....	....
....	....

The properties of covalent compounds	Substances tested that had these properties
....	....
....	....
....	....

Evaluation

5   The test for solubility was qualitative (the result was a yes or no answer). How could you modify the test to get quantitative (numerical value) data?

....

....

6   The test for conductivity was qualitative (the bulb was either lit or not lit). How could you modify the test to get quantitative (numerical value) data?

....

....

7 How might the temperature of the water you used have affected solubility?

....

....

8 One of the substances did not fit into the Venn diagram in Figure 3.5. Do you think this substance is ionic or covalent? Give reasons for your choice.

....

....

....

....

REFLECTION

Many practicals require you to work in pairs or larger groups. Think about how you organised your group when performing the different tests.

What problems did you encounter?

What improvements could you have made to the organisation?

How will you implement these improvements in future practicals?

EXAM-STYLE QUESTIONS

1 Two students are trying to decide if a newly discovered compound is ionic or covalent. Plan an investigation to determine which type of compound it is.

....

....

....

....

.... [6]

CONTINUED

2   Magnesium is a very reactive metal that burns in air to form a white powder.

COMMAND WORD

identify: name/ select/recognise

a   Look at the diagram below and **identify** the apparatus used for burning magnesium.

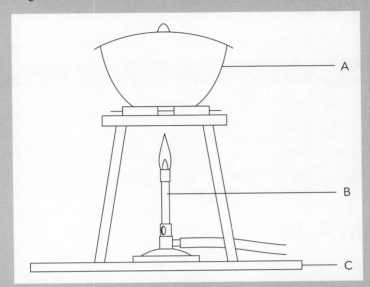

A: ....

B: ....

C: ....   **[3]**

b   On the diagram, draw an arrow to show where the magnesium should be placed.   **[1]**

c   What is the name of the gas that magnesium reacts with in the air?

....   **[1]**

d   **Suggest** one safety precaution that you would take during this experiment.

....
....   **[1]**

e   **Describe** how you could compare the mass of the contents of the crucible before and after the experiment.

....
....
....   **[3]**

[Total: 9]

COMMAND WORDS

suggest: apply knowledge and understanding to situations where there are a range of valid responses in order to make proposals/ put forward considerations

describe: state the points of a topic / give characteristics and main features

> Chapter 4
Chemical formulae and equations

THE INVESTIGATIONS IN THIS CHAPTER WILL:

- use models to help understand the chemical formulae of compounds

- show how to deduce the formula of a compound from a model

- identify reactants and products in a chemical reaction

- enable you to practise writing word and symbol equations, including state symbols.

Practical investigation 4.1: Deducing chemical formulae

KEY WORDS

chemical formula: a shorthand method of representing chemical elements and compounds using the symbols of the elements

IN THIS INVESTIGATION YOU WILL:

- use models to identify the atoms that make up various compounds

- use the numbers of each type of atom to determine the chemical formula of a compound.

YOU WILL NEED:

- models of eight different compounds provided by your teacher.

Getting started

You will be using models to show chemical formulae.

Fill in the tables to show which element each colour represents in the models.

Element	Colour of model atom
Hydrogen	
Carbon	
Oxygen	

Element	Colour of model atom
Nitrogen	
Sulfur	
Chlorine	

Method

1   You will need to move to your first model station. The order in which you choose to investigate the models does not matter.

2   Identify the types of atom present in the model. Record the types of atom in the results table in the Recording data section.

3   Count the number of each type of atom in the model and record this number in the results table.

Recording data

1   Record your data in the table below.

Compound number	Types of atoms (elements) present	Number of each type of atoms (element) present
1		
2		
3		
4		
5		
6		
7		
8		

Handling data

2   Try to identify the name of each compound.

> **TIP**
>
> Some of the compounds will have names that you will need to research as they
> do not follow the usual naming pattern of compounds, e.g. water is not called
> hydrogen oxide.

Compound number	Name of compound
1	
2	
3	
4	
5	
6	
7	
8	

Analysis

3   Name two compounds that are covalent compounds.

   ....

4   Which compound is an ionic compound?

   ....

5   Which element forms the most bonds in the models?

   ....

6   Which elements form the fewest bonds in the models?

   ....

Evaluation

7   Suggest one benefit of using models that show the structure of compounds.

....

....

8   Suggest one limitation of using models to show the structure of compounds.

....

....

Practical investigation 4.2: Reactants and products

KEY WORDS

state symbols: symbols used to show the physical state of the reactants and products in a chemical reaction: they are s (solid), l (liquid), g (gas) and aq (in solution in water)

chemical symbol: a letter or group of letters representing an element in a chemical formula

word equation: a summary of a chemical reaction using the chemical names of the reactants and products

IN THIS INVESTIGATION YOU WILL:

- explore chemical reactions by making careful observations

- use both word and symbol equations to represent the reactants and products in a chemical reaction

- use state symbols to identify the state of different substances in a chemical reaction

 deduce the symbol equation with state symbols for a chemical reaction.

YOU WILL NEED:

- heat-resistant mat • Bunsen burner • crucible and lid • tripod
- clay triangle • tongs • two pieces of magnesium ribbon
- sodium hydrogen carbonate • dilute hydrochloric acid (0.5 mol/dm^3)
- dilute sulfuric acid (0.5 mol/dm^3) • spatula • test-tube rack • two boiling tubes
- two pipettes • safety glasses • lab coat • gloves.

Safety

- Do not look at magnesium when it is burning as it may harm your eyes. Wear eye protection throughout.

- Be very careful with the hot crucible and do not attempt to touch it until it has cooled down.

- Sulfuric acid and hydrochloric acid are both moderate hazards.

Getting started

In this investigation you will need to use tongs to remove the lid of a crucible. The handle on the top of a crucible lid is very small and difficult to pick up with tongs. Practise removing the lid from the crucible and replacing it using the tongs until you are confident that you are able to so.

Method

In this investigation you will be completing three different reactions. These reactions can be completed in any order. The important thing is that you make careful observations about the chemical state (solid (s), liquid (l), aqueous (aq) or gas (g)) of each reactant and product.

> **TIP**
>
> The reactants are the substances on the left-hand side of a chemical equation. The reactants 'react' with each other. The products are the substances on the right-hand side of a chemical equation. The products are 'produced' by the reactions that take place between the reactants.

Magnesium and oxygen

1   Place the tripod on the heat-resistant mat. Rest the clay triangle so that it sits securely in the middle of the tripod.

2   Take a piece of magnesium ribbon and place it into the crucible. You may need to roll the magnesium ribbon around a pencil to make the ribbon into a spiral so that it will fit in the crucible. Record magnesium as one of the reactants in your results. Also add the appropriate state symbol for magnesium.

3   Place the crucible in the clay triangle. Add the lid to the crucible.

4   Connect the Bunsen burner to the gas supply. Place the Bunsen burner under the tripod.

5   Light the Bunsen burner and turn the collar so that there is a roaring blue flame. Move the Bunsen burner so that the flame is directly under the crucible.

6   Heat the crucible with the Bunsen burner for a few minutes. Once the magnesium is hot enough it will react with the oxygen in the air. Record the chemical symbol and state symbol for oxygen in your results.

7   Using the metal tongs carefully lift the handle of the crucible lid. If the magnesium begins to burn (you will see a white flash) carefully replace the lid on the crucible. Heat for another two minutes and then remove the crucible lid again.

8   Repeat step 7 until only white ash is visible in the crucible. The white ash is actually magnesium oxide (the product of this reaction). Record the chemical symbol and state symbol for magnesium oxide in your results.

9   Turn the Bunsen burner off and allow the crucible to cool down. You may begin one of the other experiments while the crucible cools down but move the tripod to a safe place on your desk.

Hydrochloric acid and sodium hydrogen carbonate

1   Place a boiling tube into the test-tube rack.

2   Using the spatula add a small amount of sodium hydrogen carbonate to the boiling tube (two or three spatulas should be enough). Sodium hydrogen carbonate ($NaHCO_3$) is one of the reactants in this experiment. Record the chemical symbol and state symbol for sodium hydrogen carbonate in your results.

3   Using a pipette collect around $3\,cm^3$ of the dilute hydrochloric acid. Hydrochloric acid (HCl) is one of the reactants in this experiment. Record the chemical symbol and state symbol for dilute hydrochloric acid in your results.

> **TIP**
>
> 'Dilute' means that a substance has had water added to it.

4   Add the hydrochloric acid to the sodium hydrogen carbonate in the boiling tube. Watch the reaction closely. You should see bubbles being given off (effervescence). These bubbles are carbon dioxide. Carbon dioxide is one of the products of this reaction. Record the chemical symbol and state symbol for carbon dioxide in your results.

5   You will not be able to see sodium chloride in the boiling tube because it is dissolved in water. Sodium chloride is one of the products of this reaction. Record the chemical symbol and state symbol for sodium chloride in your results.

6   The final product of the reaction between hydrochloric acid and sodium hydrogen carbonate is water. You will be able to see water in the boiling tube. Record the chemical symbol and state symbol for water in your results.

Sulfuric acid and magnesium

1   Place a clean boiling tube in the test-tube rack.

2   Using a clean pipette add approximately $10\,cm^3$ of dilute sulfuric acid to the boiling tube. Sulfuric acid (H_2SO_4) is one of the reactants of this reaction. Record the chemical symbol and state symbol for sulfuric acid in your results.

3   Take a piece of magnesium ribbon. Record magnesium as one of the reactants in your results. Also add the appropriate state symbol for magnesium.

4   Add the magnesium ribbon to the sulfuric acid in the boiling tube. Watch the reaction closely. You should see bubbles being given off. These bubbles are hydrogen, one of the products of this reaction. Record the chemical symbol and state symbol for hydrogen in your results.

5   You will not be able to see magnesium sulfate in the boiling tube because magnesium sulfate is dissolved in water. Magnesium sulfate ($MgSO_4$) is one of the products of this reaction. Record the chemical symbol and state symbol for magnesium sulfate in your results.

Recording data

1 Record your data in the tables below.

Magnesium and oxygen

Substance	Symbol	State
Magnesium		
Oxygen		
Magnesium oxide		

Hydrochloric acid and sodium hydrogen carbonate

Substance	Symbol	State
Sodium hydrogen carbonate		
Hydrochloric acid		
Carbon dioxide		
Sodium chloride		
Water		

Sulfuric acid and magnesium

Substance	Symbol	State
Sulfuric acid		
Magnesium		
Hydrogen		
Magnesium sulfate		

Analysis

2   Using the names of each of the products and reactants you have recorded, write the balanced word equations for each reaction.

    a   Magnesium and oxygen:

    .... + ... → ....

    b   Hydrochloric acid and sodium hydrogen carbonate:

    .... + ... →

    .... + ... + ...

    c   Sulfuric acid and magnesium:

    .... + ... → .... + ...

3   Also deduce the symbol equation with state symbols for each reaction.

    a   Magnesium and oxygen:

    .... (......) + ... (......) → .... (......)

    b   Hydrochloric acid and sodium hydrogen carbonate:

    .... (......) + ... (......) →

    .... (......) + ... (......) + ... (......)

> **TIP**
>
> When water itself is produced in a reaction, it has the symbol (l) for liquid, not (aq) for aqueous.

    c   Sulfuric acid and magnesium

    .... (......) + ... (......) →

    .... (......) + ... (......)

Evaluation

4   When hydrochloric acid was reacted with sodium hydrogen carbonate, the product sodium chloride was produced. Sodium chloride dissolves in water to form an aqueous solution and is therefore not visible. Suggest how the sodium chloride could have been separated from the water.

....

....

5 The magnesium ribbon was reacted with the oxygen in the air. Suggest why the magnesium ribbon was heated in a crucible for this reaction instead of simply holding the magnesium ribbon in tongs and heating directly in the Bunsen burner flame.

....

....

REFLECTION

Many practicals require you to perform a series of tests. Are you confident in performing these?

How could you improve your organisation when performing such tests and recording different sets of observations?

....

....

....

EXAM-STYLE QUESTIONS

1 Two students are building models of compounds. They have a molecular modelling kit containing three types of atoms (red, blue and green) and some links to represent bonds. They have enough of each coloured model atoms to make any substances they choose to.

a **Suggest** how the students could make a model of a water molecule.

....

....

.... **[3]**

b Suggest how the students could make a model of a carbon dioxide molecule.

....

....

.... **[3]**

COMMAND WORD

suggest: apply knowledge and understanding to situations where there are a range of valid responses in order to make proposals/ put forward considerations

CONTINUED

c   One of the students states the following: 'It is not possible to make a model of an ethanol (C_2H_5OH) molecule with the equipment available.' **Explain** why the student is wrong.

....

....

.... [3]

[Total: 9]

COMMAND WORD

explain: set out purposes or reasons / make the relationships between things evident / provide why and/or how and support with relevant evidence

2   A student is conducting an experiment to make sodium chloride. They add dilute hydrochloric acid to dilute sodium hydroxide, which react to produce sodium chloride and water.

a   Write the word equation and add state symbols to the symbol equation.

.... + ... →

.... + ...

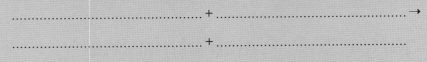

$HCl(......) + NaOH(......) \rightarrow NaCl(......) + H_2O(......)$ [3]

The student heated the sodium chloride solution until all of the water evaporated.

b   Add the state symbols to the sodium chloride and water after heating.

$NaCl(......) + H_2O(......)$ [1]

Look at the chemical equation in part **a**.

c   List the reactants and products in the reaction

Reactants:

....

Products:

.... [2]

[Total: 6]

> Chapter 5
Chemical calculations

Whilst some learning intentions included within this chapter are Core, these practical investigations are intended for students who are studying the Supplement content of the syllabus.

THE INVESTIGATIONS IN THIS CHAPTER WILL:

> explore the concept of the mole and use the mole in calculations

> use empirical formulae of compounds in calculations

> calculate percentage yield, reacting masses, limiting reagents, and volumes of gases and solutions

> develop your understanding of the term 'relative atomic mass'.

Practical investigation 5.1: Calculating the ratio of water in hydrated salts

KEY WORDS

empirical formula: a formula for a compound that shows the simplest ratio of atoms present

TIP

The branch of chemistry involving calculations based on relative masses, moles and ratios is known as quantitative chemistry.

IN THIS INVESTIGATION YOU WILL:

> understand the term 'empirical formula'

• make and record precise and repeated measurements

> calculate empirical and molecular formulae from the data collected.

YOU WILL NEED:

• two crucibles with lids • tongs • tripod • clay triangle • Bunsen burner
• heat-resistant mat • copper(II) sulfate • magnesium sulfate • two watch glasses
• spatula • safety glasses • lab coat • gloves • balance.

Safety

- Do not leave the investigation unattended when the Bunsen burner is on.

- Remember to use the safety flame when not actively using the Bunsen burner.

- The crucible will get very hot, so use the tongs to move the crucible and let it cool before you take measurements.

- Copper(II) sulfate is a moderate hazard and harmful to the aquatic environment. Waste from experiments using copper(II) sulfate must not be poured down the drain.

- Wear eye protection throughout.

Getting started

You will be making repeated measurements using a balance. Make sure you are familiar with how to read a balance. You will be using a balance that is precise to two decimal places (0.01 g). Why do you think this precision is needed?

....

....

Method

1 Take one of the crucibles and weigh the crucible on the balance. Add four spatulas of magnesium sulfate to the crucible. Reweigh the crucible and record the data in the table in the Recording data section.

2 Set up the tripod and clay triangle. Place the crucible in the clay triangle and heat the crucible on a blue Bunsen flame for around five minutes. The lid can be used to cover the crucible temporarily if the magnesium sulfate starts to spit. The lid should be removed once the spitting stops.

3 Remove the crucible from the clay triangle using the tongs and place the crucible on the heat-resistant mat. Allow the crucible to cool, but place a watch glass on top of the crucible to prevent the reabsorption of water.

4 While waiting for the first crucible to cool, repeat steps 1–3 with copper(II) sulfate.

5 Return the crucible with magnesium sulfate to the clay triangle and heat for a second time, but only for three minutes. Remove the crucible from the heat and allow it to cool. Repeat this step with copper(II) sulfate.

6 Reweigh both crucibles. Repeat step 5 until a constant mass is achieved (there are extra rows in the table where you can record this data).

   Your teacher might suggest the use of a desiccator (a device for drying material) to dry the salts instead of repeated heating.

Recording data

1 Record your data in the table.

	Magnesium sulfate	Copper(II) sulfate
Mass of crucible / g		
Mass of crucible and salt / g		
Mass of crucible and salt after heating first time / g		
Mass of crucible and salt after heating second time / g		
Mass of crucible and salt after heating repeat reading / g		
Mass of crucible and salt after heating repeat reading / g		
Constant mass of crucible and salt / g		

Handling data

You will now need to use the data from your results to complete some calculations.

TIP
Make sure to copy data from the results table accurately.

2 Use the data from the results table to complete the following:

Mass of magnesium sulfate at start: ....g

Mass of magnesium sulfate at end: ....g

Mass of water lost: ....g

Mass of copper(II) sulfate at start: ....g

Mass of copper(II) sulfate at end: ....g

Mass of water lost: ....g

Analysis

3 The empirical formula for anhydrous magnesium sulfate is $MgSO_4$.

How many moles of magnesium sulfate did you have at the end of the investigation?

(A_r: O = 16, Mg = 24, S = 32)

....

....

4 How many moles of water were lost from the magnesium sulfate during the investigation?
(A_r: H = 1, O = 16)

....

....

5 What was the ratio of magnesium sulfate to water?

....

6 The empirical formula for anhydrous copper(II) sulfate is $CuSO_4$. How many moles of copper(II) sulfate did you have at the end of the investigation?
(A_r: O = 16, S = 32, Cu = 64)

....

....

7 How many moles of water were lost from the copper(II) sulfate during the investigation?
(A_r: H = 1, O = 16)

....

8 What was the ratio of copper(II) sulfate to water?

....

9 Think about any sources of error in this investigation. What improvements could you suggest?

....

....

....

....

REFLECTION

Calculations are an important part of quantitative chemistry. Think about your maths skills. Were you confident applying your skills to the calculations in this investigation?

Which aspects did you find easy and which parts did you find difficult?

....

....

....

Practical investigation 5.2: Calculating percentage yield using copper(II) carbonate

KEY WORDS

mole: the measure of amount of substance in chemistry; 1 mole of a substance has a mass equal to its relative formula mass in grams – that amount of substance contains 6.02×10^{23} (the Avogadro constant) atoms, molecules or formula units depending on the substance considered

percentage yield: a measure of the actual yield of a reaction when carried out experimentally compared to the theoretical yield calculated from the equation:

$$\text{percentage yield} = \frac{\text{actual yield}}{\text{predicted yield}} \times 100$$

relative formula mass (M_r): the sum of all the relative atomic masses of the atoms present in a 'formula unit' of a substance (see also **relative molecular mass**)

relative molecular mass (M_r): the sum of all the relative atomic masses of the atoms present in a molecule (see also **relative formula mass**)

thermal decomposition: the breakdown of a compound due to heating

IN THIS INVESTIGATION YOU WILL:

- compare the expected and actual values for the products produced by the thermal decomposition of copper(II) carbonate

> calculate the percentage yield

- use values from different groups to calculate a mean.

YOU WILL NEED:

- crucible • tripod • clay triangle • Bunsen burner • heat-resistant mat
- copper(II) carbonate • tongs • spatula • measuring cylinder • safety glasses
- lab coat • gloves • balance.

Safety

- Copper(II) carbonate is harmful if swallowed and is harmful to the aquatic environment. Waste from experiments using copper(II) carbonate must not be poured down the drain.

- The crucible will get very hot so take care to allow adequate time for the crucible to cool before you touch it.

- Wear eye protection throughout.

Getting started

The total amount of product actually produced by a reaction is not always the same as the expected amount predicted by the chemical equation. Can you think of some reasons why this is possible and reasons for the difference?

....

....

> **TIP**
>
> The expected yield is also known as the theoretical or predicted yield.

Method

1 Weigh the crucible. Record the mass of the crucible in your results table. You will need to design your data collection table in the Recording data section.

2 Add five spatulas of copper(II) carbonate to the crucible and then reweigh the crucible. Record the mass of the crucible with the copper(II) carbonate in your results table.

3 Set up the tripod and clay triangle on the heat-resistant mat.

4 Place the crucible in the clay triangle and then heat the crucible using the Bunsen burner on a cool blue flame.

5 Observe the copper(II) carbonate. Stop heating the crucible when all of the copper(II) carbonate powder has changed colour from green to black.

6 Using the spatula, carefully stir the copper(II) carbonate powder to make sure there is no green colour remaining. If there is any green colour, heat the copper(II) carbonate powder for a few more minutes. Stop heating once all of the copper(II) carbonate powder has changed from green to black.

7 Use the tongs to move the crucible to the heat-resistant mat and allow the crucible to cool.

8 Reweigh the crucible on the balance after the crucible has cooled. Record the mass of the crucible with the powder in your results table.

Recording data

1   Design a table to record the results of your investigation. To get more reliable data it would be useful to include results from at least three other groups.

TIP
Include a column for the mean results in your results table.

Handling data

2   Use the data from the results table to complete the following:

Mass of crucible: ......g

Mass of crucible and copper(II) carbonate: ......g

Mass of copper(II) carbonate at the start of the investigation: ......g (= mass of crucible and copper(II) carbonate – mass of crucible)

Mass of crucible and copper oxide at the end: ......g

Mass of copper oxide at the end of the investigation: ......g (= mass of crucible and copper oxide at the end – mass of crucible)

Analysis

3 What is the molar mass of copper(II) carbonate ($CuCO_3$)?
(A_r: C = 12, O = 16, Cu = 64)

....

4 What is the molar mass of copper oxide (CuO)?
(A_r: O = 16, Cu = 64)

....

5 Calculate how many moles of copper(II) carbonate you had, by dividing the mass you measured by the molar mass.

$$\frac{\text{actual mass}}{\text{molar mass}} = \text{number of moles}$$

> **TIP**
>
> The molar mass is the mass, in grams, of 1 mole of a substance.

$$\frac{\dots\dots\text{g}}{\dots\dots\text{g/mol}} = \dots\dots\text{mol}$$

6 The number of moles of copper oxide produced should be the same as the number of moles of copper(II) carbonate reacted. Calculate the expected yield by multiplying the number of moles of copper(II) carbonate you reacted by the molar mass of copper oxide.

Number of moles of copper(II) carbonate × molar mass of copper oxide = expected yield

..........mol × ....g/mol = ...g

7 Now calculate percentage yield. To do this, you must divide your actual yield (the recorded mass of copper oxide) by the expected yield.

$$\frac{\text{actual yield}}{\text{expected yield}} \times 100 = \text{percentage yield}$$

$$\frac{\dots\dots\text{g}}{\dots\dots\text{g}} \times 100 = \dots\dots\%$$

Evaluation

8 What was the difference between the expected and actual yield?

..........%

9 What can the difference between the percentage yield and actual yield tell you about the method that you used?

....

Practical investigation 5.3: Calculating the relative atomic mass of magnesium

KEY WORDS

relative atomic mass (A_r): the average mass of naturally occurring atoms of an element on a scale where the carbon-12 atom has a mass of exactly 12 units

IN THIS INVESTIGATION YOU WILL:

> learn how to calculate the relative atomic mass of magnesium

• use techniques for accurately measuring the volume of a gas.

YOU WILL NEED:

• two beakers (100 cm³ and 250 cm³) • burette • clamp stand and burette clamp
• small funnel • abrasive paper, such as emery paper • magnesium ribbon
• dilute hydrochloric acid (2.0 mol/dm³) • distilled water • measuring cylinder
• safety glasses • lab coat • gloves • balance.

Safety

• Report any spills to your teacher.

• Hydrochloric acid is a moderate hazard.

• Wear eye protection throughout.

Getting started

Figure 5.1 shows diagrams of the cross-section of a burette valve. Draw on the diagrams to show how the burette valve will appear when the valve is in the open position (left) and how the burette valve will appear when the valve is in the closed position (right).

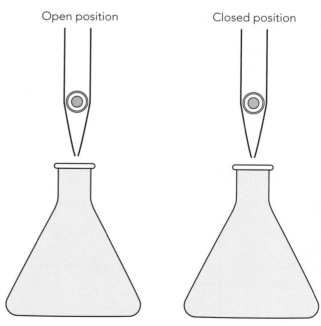

Figure 5.1: Burette valve.

Method

1   Rub the abrasive paper on the magnesium ribbon until the magnesium ribbon is shiny. Weigh the piece of magnesium ribbon on the balance. Record the mass of magnesium to three decimal places.

2   Using a funnel, carefully pour 25 cm³ of hydrochloric acid into the burette. Add 25 cm³ of distilled water to the burette. Add the distilled water very slowly so that the mixing of liquids is limited.

> **TIP**
>
> Always check that the burette tap is closed before adding liquids.

3   Press the magnesium ribbon into the top of the burette. This should be done on the longest side so that the magnesium ribbon bends. The magnesium ribbon needs to be pressed against the sides of the burette glass. The magnesium must not touch the water and should be firmly embedded in place (Figure 5.2).

4   Half fill the 250 cm³ beaker with distilled water. Quickly invert the burette. Place the open end of the burette under the surface of the water in the beaker (Figure 5.2). Clamp the burette to the stand. Take a reading of the water level and record the data in the table in the Recording data section.

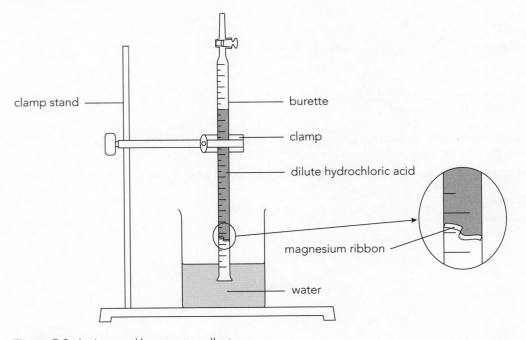

Figure 5.2: An inverted burette to collect gas.

5   Allow the acid and magnesium to react. The reaction is finished when the liquid level remains constant and no more gas is produced. Record the level of liquid in the burette in the table.

Recording data

1 Mass of magnesium = ... g

2 Record your data in the table below.

Burette reading at start of investigation / cm³	Burette reading at end of investigation / cm³	Volume of gas produced / cm³

Handling data

3 Using your data, calculate the number of moles of hydrogen gas in your sample.

The molar gas volume (the volume occupied by 1 mole of any gas) is 24 dm³ at 25 °C.

To calculate how many moles of hydrogen were produced, divide the volume of gas produced by the molar gas volume.

$$\text{Number of moles of hydrogen} = \frac{\text{volume of hydrogen produced (dm}^3)}{24\ \text{dm}^3/\text{mol}}$$

You will first need to convert the volume of hydrogen gas produced from cm³ to dm³ (1 dm³ = 1000 cm³).

$$\begin{aligned}\text{Volume of hydrogen produced} \\ \text{(from Results table)}\end{aligned} = \frac{..........\ \text{cm}^3}{1000} = ... \ \text{dm}^3$$

$$\text{Number of moles of hydrogen} = \frac{..........\ \text{dm}^3}{24\ \text{dm}^3/\text{mol}} = ... \ \text{mol}$$

4 The formula for calculating relative atomic mass is given below. In the space provided add your own data to calculate the relative atomic mass of magnesium.

For every 1 mole of hydrogen produced, 1 mole of magnesium has dissolved in the acid.

$$\frac{\text{mass of magnesium}}{\text{number of moles of magnesium}} = \text{relative atomic mass of magnesium}$$

$$\frac{..........\ \text{g}}{..........\ \text{mol}} = ...\text{g}/\text{mol}$$

Evaluation

5 To calculate the number of moles of hydrogen gas produced, you used the figure of 24 dm³ for the volume of gas occupied by 1 mole of a gas. Which two variables affect the volume occupied by 1 mole of gas?

....

....

6   How could you have taken readings to take account of these variables?

   ....

   ....

7   How could you have improved your experiment to make your results more accurate?

   ....

   ....

8   How could you have made your results more reliable?

   ....

   ....

REFLECTION

Think about what you know about the mole. Did using the mole in actual calculations help you to understand the concept?

What strategies could you use to explain the relationship between moles, mass and numbers of atoms or molecules to your partner?

   ....

   ....

Practical investigation 5.4: Finding the empirical formula of copper oxide

IN THIS INVESTIGATION YOU WILL:

> deduce the empirical formula of a compound from experimental data

- make careful measurements
- collect quantitative and qualitative data.

YOU WILL NEED:

- rubber tubing   • heat-resistant mat   • spatula
- reduction tube (glass test-tube with a small hole at the closed end)
- clamp stand and clamp   • Bunsen burner
- stopper with a hole and glass tube attachment   • balance   • copper(II) oxide
- safety glasses   • lab coat   • gloves.

Safety

- Methane is flammable; take care when lighting the gas from the reduction tube.

- Wear eye protection throughout.

- Copper(II) oxide is corrosive, a moderate hazard and harmful to the aquatic environment. Waste from experiments using copper(II) oxide must not be poured down the drain.

Getting started

Review the equipment needed for this investigation. In the space provided, record the function and draw a diagram of each piece of equipment.

Reduction tube Function:	**Diagram**
Bunsen burner Function:	**Diagram**

Method

1 Use the balance to weigh the reduction tube with the stopper and glass tube attached. Record the data in the table in the Recording data section.

2 Open the stopper and carefully add two spatulas of copper(II) oxide to the reduction tube. Reweigh the reduction tube. Record the data in the table in the Recording data section.

3 Clamp the reduction tube to the clamp stand and attach the rubber tubing to the glass tube (Figure 5.3).

4 Place the Bunsen burner on the heat-resistant mat and connect the Bunsen burner to the gas supply. Ensure that the Bunsen burner is directly underneath the copper(II) oxide powder in the reduction tube.

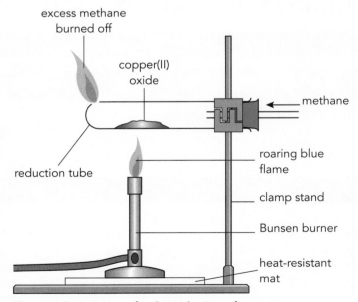

Figure 5.3: Apparatus for the reduction of copper.

5   Connect the end of the rubber tubing attached to the reduction tube to the methane supply.

6   Turn on the methane supply to the reduction tube. Wait ten seconds and then hold a lit splint next to the small hole at the end of reduction tube. The flame should ignite.

7   Light the Bunsen burner and turn the collar so that there is a roaring blue flame.

8   Move the Bunsen burner so that the flame touches every part of the copper(II) oxide. All parts of the copper(II) oxide must be heated for the reaction to take place.

> ### TIP
> Do not heat the reduction tube too strongly near to the stopper as this could cause the stopper to burn and start producing smoke.

9   Observe the colour change in the copper(II) oxide. Heat for a further three minutes after the powder turns orange–copper colour and then turn off the Bunsen burner.

10   Allow the reduction tube to cool, but keep the methane supply passing over the product so that the copper does not react with oxygen in the atmosphere.

11   Switch off the methane supply to the reduction tube after the tube has cooled.

12   Weigh the reduction tube with the stopper and record the final mass in the table. This final mass will include the mass of copper produced.

Recording data

1   Record your data in the table below.

Mass of reduction tube and stopper / g	
Mass of reduction tube, stopper and copper(II) oxide / g	
Mass of reduction tube, stopper and copper / g	

Handling data

2   Use the data you recorded to calculate the starting mass of copper(II) oxide and the mass of copper produced.

Mass of copper(II) oxide / g	
Mass of copper / g	

Assuming the mass of copper in the sample remains the same, calculate the mass of oxygen that was lost from the copper(II) oxide.

Mass of copper(II) oxide − mass copper = mass of oxygen lost

.... g − .... g = ... g

Analysis

3 To calculate the number of moles of each element the mass must be divided by the relative atomic mass.

The relative atomic mass of copper is 64.

The relative atomic mass of oxygen is 16.

Number of moles of copper: ....

Number of moles of oxygen: ....

To find the ratio divide the number of moles of each element by the smallest number.

What is the ratio of copper to oxygen in copper oxide?

....

4 Use your answer to question **3** to deduce the empirical formula of copper oxide.

....

Evaluation

5 What were the sources of error in this investigation?

....

....

6 How could you have obtained more accurate data for this investigation?

....

....

EXAM-STYLE QUESTIONS

1 Two students are trying to calculate the relative atomic mass of magnesium experimentally. They react the magnesium with dilute hydrochloric acid in an inverted burette. The magnesium is allowed to react with the hydrochloric acid and a gas is produced. Once no more gas is produced, the reaction is complete.

a Look at the burette readings in the figure below. Record the readings at the start and the end of the reaction in the table.

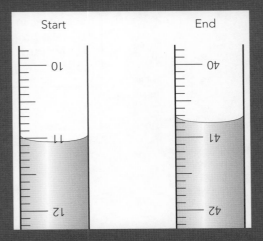

Burette reading at start of investigation / cm³	Burette reading at end of investigation / cm³	Volume of gas produced / cm³
i .... [1]	ii .... [1]	.... [1]

COMMAND WORD

calculate: work out from given facts, figures or information

b **Calculate** the volume of gas produced in this reaction. Add this value to the table.

c Calculate the number of moles of hydrogen gas produced

$$\text{Number of moles of hydrogen} = \frac{\text{volume of hydrogen produced (dm}^3)}{24\,\text{dm}^3/\text{mol}}$$

Volume of hydrogen produced = ... dm³ (to 4 d.p.)

Number of moles of hydrogen gas = ... mol [2]

d One mole of Magnesium reacts to produce 1 mole of hydrogen gas. The mass of magnesium used was 0.029 g. Use this information to calculate the relative atomic mass of magnesium.

A_r magnesium = ... [2]

[Total: 7]

CONTINUED

2   The shell of a bird's egg is made mostly from calcium carbonate. A student wanted to calculate what percentage of calcium carbonate a bird's eggshell contains. **Suggest** a method he could use to do this.

....

....

....

....

....

....

.... [9]

COMMAND WORD

suggest: apply knowledge and understanding to situations where there are a range of valid responses in order to make proposals/ put forward considerations

3   Two students are attempting to determine the relative formula mass for magnesium oxide. They weighed a piece of magnesium. The mass of the magnesium was 1.255 g. They also weighed a crucible and lid, which had a mass of 45.653 g.

They need to heat the crucible to a high temperature using a Bunsen burner for the magnesium to react with oxygen.

a   i   Suggest which type of Bunsen flame they should use to heat the crucible.

.... [1]

ii   Suggest why they need to use a lid with the crucible when heating the magnesium.

.... [1]

b   After reacting magnesium with oxygen, the new mass of magnesium oxide and the crucible with the lid was 48.153 g.

i   Using this information calculate the mass of magnesium oxide.
Mass magnesium oxide = ... g   [1]

ii   Use the initial mass of magnesium used to calculate the mass of oxygen in the magnesium oxide produced.
Mass of oxygen in magnesium oxide = ... g   [2]

iii   **Deduce** the ratio of magnesium atoms to oxygen atoms in magnesium oxide.

....

.... [2]

[Total: 7]

COMMAND WORD

deduce: conclude from available information

Chapter 6

Electrochemistry

THE INVESTIGATIONS IN THIS CHAPTER WILL:

- show that electrolysis is used to obtain products that can be very valuable and that there are some substances that can be very difficult to obtain in any other way

- explore why copper is extracted using electrolysis

- extract very pure copper using the process of electrolysis.

> Practical investigation 6.1: The electrolysis of copper

KEY WORDS

anode: the electrode in any type of cell at which oxidation (the loss of electrons) takes place – in electrolysis it is the positive electrode

cathode: the electrode in any type of cell at which reduction (the gain of electrons) takes place; in electrolysis it is the negative electrode

electrolysis: the breakdown of an ionic compound, molten or in aqueous solution, by the use of electricity

electrolyte: an ionic compound that will conduct electricity when it is molten or dissolved in water; electrolytes will not conduct electricity when solid

ions: charged particles made from an atom, or groups of atoms (compound ions), by the loss or gain of electrons

variable: any factor in an *experiment* that can be changed (independent variable), measured (dependent variable) or controlled (controlled variable)

IN THIS INVESTIGATION YOU WILL:

- define electrolysis and the components of simple electrolytic cells

- > determine electrode products for the electrolysis of aqueous copper(II) sulfate using copper electrodes.

YOU WILL NEED:

- beaker (250 cm³) • two copper electrodes • clamp stand and clamp
- 6V DC power supply • leads and crocodile clips • copper(II) sulfate solution
(0.5 mol/dm³) • steel nail • safety glasses • lab coat • gloves • balance.

Safety

- Ensure that the electrodes do not touch as this will create a short circuit.

- Copper(II) sulfate is a moderate hazard and harmful to the aquatic environment. Waste from experiments using copper(II) sulfate must not be poured down the drain.

Getting started

Copper has many uses. Discuss with your partner how the properties of copper relate to its different uses. Where might you need to use very pure copper?

....

....

Method

1   Pour 150 cm³ of copper(II) sulfate solution into the beaker.

2   Mark one copper electrode with the letter **A** and the other copper electrode with the letter **B** at one end. Weigh each electrode and record the mass of each electrode in the results table in the Recording data section.

> **TIP**
>
> It is best to use a steel nail to scratch the letters into the surface of the pieces of copper. Any ink is likely to be dissolved or covered up with copper.

3   Use the clamp stand to secure the two copper electrodes so that the electrodes are partially submerged in the copper(II) sulfate solution. Connect the crocodile clips and leads to the power supply, but do not switch on the power supply. Ensure that your copper electrodes are not touching. See Figure 6.1.

4   Make sure the power supply is set for 6 V and then switch on the power supply.

5   Allow the reaction to run for 30 minutes.

6   Turn off the power supply. Carefully remove the copper electrodes from the solution. Allow the electrodes to dry naturally for five minutes. Do not use a paper towel to dry the electrodes.

7   Reweigh the copper electrodes.

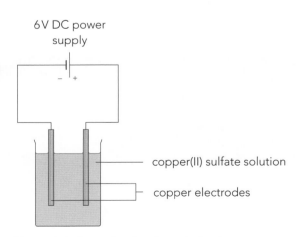

Figure 6.1: Setup for the electrolysis of copper.

Recording data

1 Record your data in the results table.

Electrode	Mass at start of experiment / g	Mass at end of experiment / g	Change in mass / g
A			
B			

Handling data

2 What was the difference between the change in mass of electrode **A** and electrode **B**?

....

Analysis

3 From the data, decide which of the two electrodes was the anode and which was the cathode. Give reasons for your answers.

....

....

....

....

Evaluation

4 Why did you air-dry the copper electrodes rather than using a paper towel to dry them?

....

5 What was the purpose of the electrolyte (copper(II) sulfate solution)?

....

....

6 Explain why the mass lost by the anode was greater than the mass gained by the cathode.

....

....

7 How would the results have been different if graphite electrodes had been used instead of copper electrodes?

....

....

Practical investigation 6.2: Electroplating

KEY WORD

electroplating: a process of electrolysis in which a metal object is coated (plated) with a layer of another metal

IN THIS INVESTIGATION YOU WILL:

- learn how metals are electroplated
- identify and change an independent variable
- analyse results to draw conclusions.

YOU WILL NEED:

- zinc strip • five copper strips • ammeter • powerpack • crocodile clips
- wires • zinc sulfate solution (1.0 mol/dm³) • balance
- hydrochloric acid solution (1.0 mol/dm³) • beaker (250 cm³) • paper towel • timer
- forceps • beaker (50 cm³) • steel nail • safety glasses • lab coat • gloves.

TIP

Electroplating involves depositing a thin layer of metal onto the surface of another metal. Metal objects can be electroplated to improve their appearance and resistance to corrosion.

Safety

- Ensure that the electrodes do not touch as this will create a short circuit; do not increase the voltage higher than 6 V.
- Hydrochloric acid is a moderate hazard.
- Zinc sulfate is an irritant, is corrosive, a moderate hazard and hazardous to the aquatic environment. Waste from experiments using zinc sulfate must not be poured down the drain.
- Wear eye protection throughout.

Getting started

You will be given a choice of two different methods in this investigation and will therefore need to choose which variable you change. Look at the Practical skills and support section at the start of this workbook and ensure you are familiar with the different types of variable (independent variable, dependent variable and control variable).

Method

You may change either the current in the circuit or the time that the plating reaction takes place for. Both methods are described.

Current

1 Using the steel nail scratch the numbers 1–5 onto your copper strips so that you know which strip you are testing.

2 Add 250 cm³ of zinc sulfate to the beaker.

3 Check that the power supply is switched off. Attach wires to the positive and negative terminals of the power supply. Attach the end of the wire connected to the negative terminal to the ammeter.

4 Attach another wire to the ammeter and then attach a crocodile clip to the other end of this wire.

5 Attach a crocodile clip to the other end of the wire connected to the positive terminal.

6 Clip the positive wire onto the zinc strip.

7 Add 50 cm³ of hydrochloric acid to the 50 cm³ beaker.

8 Place the first copper strip that you have labelled '1' into the hydrochloric acid for one minute. Ensure that the whole strip is covered by the hydrochloric acid. Remove the copper strip using the forceps and dry the copper strip on a paper towel.

9 Place the copper strip on the balance and record the mass to three decimal places. Record the reading in your results table. You will need to design your data collection table in the Recording data section.

10 Clip the crocodile clip attached to the ammeter to the copper strip.

11 Lower both the zinc strip and the copper strip into the zinc sulfate. Ensure that both strips of metal are at least half covered by the zinc sulfate solution.

12 Set the power supply to the lowest setting and then turn on the power supply.

13 Increase the power supply until the ammeter reads approximately 0.8 A.

14 Start the timer and allow the reaction to run for five minutes.

15 After five minutes, turn the powerpack off and remove the copper strip from the zinc sulfate solution.

16 Allow the copper strip to dry for a few minutes and then weigh the copper strip on the balance. Record the reading in your results table.

17 Repeat steps 7–10 with the next copper strip.

18 Turn the powerpack on and increase the voltage of the power supply until the ammeter reads approximately 1 A. Then repeat steps 13–15.

19 Repeat for the remaining copper strips at the approximate current values 1.2 A, 1.4 A and 1.6 A.

Time

1   Using the steel nail scratch the numbers 1–5 onto your copper strips so that you know which strip you are testing.

2   Add 250 cm³ of zinc sulfate to the beaker.

3   Check that the power supply is switched off. Attach wires to the positive and negative terminals of the power supply. Attach the end of the wire connected to the negative terminal to the ammeter.

4   Attach another wire to the ammeter and then attach a crocodile clip to the other end of this wire.

5   Attach a crocodile clip to the other end of the wire connected to the positive terminal.

6   Clip the positive wire onto the zinc strip.

7   Add 50 cm³ of hydrochloric acid to the 50 cm³ beaker.

8   Place the first copper strip that you have labelled as '1' into the hydrochloric acid for one minute. Remove the copper strip using the forceps and dry the copper strip on a paper towel.

9   Place the copper strip on the balance and record the mass to three decimal places. Record the reading in your results table.

10   Clip the crocodile clip attached to the ammeter to the copper strip.

11   Lower both the zinc strip and the copper strip into the zinc sulfate. Ensure that both strips of metal are at least half covered by the zinc sulfate solution.

12   Set the power supply to the lowest setting and then turn on the power supply.

13   Increase the power supply until the ammeter reads approximately 1.5 A.

14   Start the timer and allow the reaction to run for one minute.

15   After one minute, turn the powerpack off and remove the copper strip from the zinc sulfate solution.

16   Allow the copper strip to dry for a few minutes and then weigh the copper strip on the balance. Record the reading in your results table.

17   Repeat steps 7–10 with the next copper strip.

18   Turn the powerpack on and increase the length of time that the powerpack is turned on for to two minutes. Then repeat steps 12–15.

19   Repeat for the remaining copper strips for three, four and five minutes.

> TIP
>
> Do not use a paper towel to dry the copper strip after the copper strip has been plated. You might rub off the plating and this would affect your results.

Recording data

1   In the space provided, draw a suitable results table to record your data. Remember you will need
    to include space for the mass of the copper strips before and after the strips have been plated.

Handling data

2   a   For each of your five copper strips you must calculate the change in mass and record this
        in the table below.

Copper strip number	Independent variable value	Change in mass / g
1		
2		
3		
4		
5		

b Plot a graph to compare your independent variable (current or time) with your dependent variable (change in mass).

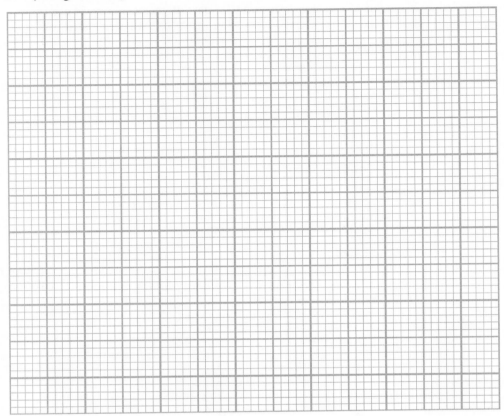

Analysis

3 Describe the pattern shown by your results.

....

....

4 Explain why changing the independent variable had the effect on the dependent variable that you observed.

....

....

Evaluation

5 State the two variables you controlled in this investigation.

....

....

....

6 Identify a variable that you did not control in your investigation.

....

7 Suggest a way you could control this variable.

....

....

8 How could you have obtained more reliable data?

....

....

REFLECTION

Do you understand the concept of variables and how they can affect the design of an experiment?

What strategy did you use to choose the variable that you decided to change in this investigation?

Do you think you can apply similar strategies to choosing variables when planning different experiments?

....

....

....

....

EXAM-STYLE QUESTIONS

1   Copper can be extracted from copper ore by reacting the ore with carbon. This is possible because carbon is more reactive than copper. When copper oxide is heated in the presence of carbon, a reduction reaction takes place. Copper can also be extracted using the process of electrolysis. Two students are investigating the electrolysis of copper using the experimental setup shown in the figure below.

a   **Identify** the anode and cathode in the diagram.

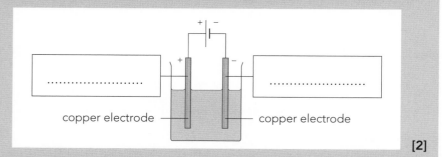

copper electrode   copper electrode

[2]

COMMAND WORDS

identify: name/ select/recognise

suggest: apply knowledge and understanding to situations where there are a range of valid responses in order to make proposals/ put forward considerations

contrast: identify/ comment on differences

b   What is the name given to the solution in an electrolytic cell? **Suggest** a suitable solution that could be used in this setup.

....

....

.... [2]

c   **Contrast** what will happen to the mass of the cathode and the anode.

....

.... [2]

d   If copper can be extracted from copper ore by using reduction, why is electrolysis also used in the production of copper?

.... [1]

e   No gas is produced during the electrolysis of copper. What could you add to the circuit to make sure that it was complete and that a reaction was taking place?

.... [1]

f   At the end of the investigation, the students found brown sludge at the bottom of the beaker. What was this and where did it come from?

.... [2]

[Total: 10]

CONTINUED

2 Two students want to purify some copper using electrolysis.

   a **Describe** a method they could use to purify copper using electrolysis.

....

....

....

....

....

....

....

.... [6]

   b **Discuss** why the mass of both electrodes changes during the reaction.

....

....

....

....

....

....

....

....

....

....

.... [8]

[Total: 14]

COMMAND WORDS

describe: state the points of a topic / give characteristics and main features

discuss: write about issue(s) or topic(s) in depth in a structured way

> # Chapter 7
Chemical energetics

THE INVESTIGATIONS IN THIS CHAPTER WILL:

- illustrate different types of chemical reactions

- show that when chemical reactions take place, energy is either taken in or given out

- examine endothermic and exothermic reactions

- explore a number of reactions with the aim of determining which are endothermic and which are exothermic.

Practical investigation 7.1:
Types of chemical reaction

KEY WORDS

combustion: a chemical reaction in which a substance reacts with oxygen – the reaction is exothermic

displacement reaction: a reaction in which a more reactive element displaces a less reactive element from a solution of its salt

photosynthesis: the chemical process by which plants synthesise glucose from atmospheric carbon dioxide and water giving off oxygen as a by-product: the energy required for the process is captured from sunlight by chlorophyll molecules in the green leaves of the plants

precipitation reaction: a reaction in which an insoluble salt is prepared from solutions of two suitable soluble salts

IN THIS INVESTIGATION YOU WILL:

- describe different types of chemical reactions by making careful measurements

- identify changes as chemical changes or physical changes

- investigate energy changes in chemical reactions using appropriate apparatus.

YOU WILL NEED:

Light

- fresh leaves (discs) or aquatic plant (*Elodea*) • boiling tube • beaker (250 cm³)
- lamp • rubber stopper • sodium hydrogen carbonate (bicarbonate of soda) • spatula.

CONTINUED

Combustion

- magnesium ribbon   • tongs   • Bunsen burner   • heat-resistant mat.

Displacement

- beaker (100 cm³)   • copper(II) sulfate solution (0.5 mol/dm³)
- measuring cylinder (50 cm³)   • two zinc strips.

Precipitation

- test-tube   • sodium chloride solution (0.2 mol/dm³)
- silver nitrate solution (0.1 mol/dm³)   • measuring cylinder (50 cm³)   • pipette.

Thermal decomposition

- test-tube   • copper(II) carbonate   • tongs   • Bunsen burner   • spatula
- heat-resistant mat.

Safety

- Stand up while performing any reactions involving heating.

- Be careful when heating the magnesium and do not look directly at the flame (your teacher may supply you with a special filter so you can observe the reaction).

- Wear eye protection throughout.

- Silver nitrate solution is a moderate hazard and harmful to the aquatic environment. Waste from experiments using silver nitrate must not be poured down the drain.

- Copper(II) sulfate is a moderate hazard and harmful to the aquatic environment. Waste from experiments using copper(II) sulfate must not be poured down the drain.

- Copper(II) carbonate is harmful if swallowed, is an irritant and is harmful to the aquatic environment. Waste from experiments using copper(II) carbonate must not be poured down the drain.

Getting started

You will be making a number of qualitative observations in this investigation. Think about the different types of reaction you have already encountered and the observations you have made. What is the difference between qualitative and quantitative observations?

....

....

Method

There are five reactions that can be completed in any order.

Photosynthesis (light)

1   Fill the beaker with water. Add one spatula of sodium hydrogen carbonate to the beaker. Stir the sodium hydrogen carbonate until it dissolves in the water.

2   Place the leaf discs or aquatic plant (*Elodea*) into the boiling tube. Fill the boiling tube to the top of the tube and seal the tube with a rubber stopper.

3   Turn the boiling tube upside down and place the boiling tube in the beaker. Remove the stopper and allow the tube to rest in the beaker for five minutes.

4   Place the lamp approximately 10 cm from the beaker and the turn on the lamp. Leave the lamp on for five minutes before making any observations.

5   Record your observations in the table in the Recording data section.

Magnesium in air (combustion)

1   Set up the Bunsen burner on the heat-resistant mat.

2   Hold the magnesium ribbon in the tongs.

3   Adjust the Bunsen burner so that is on a blue flame and then hold the magnesium ribbon in the flame. Do not look directly at the magnesium when it burns as this is dangerous.

4   Record your observations in the table in the Recording data section.

Zinc in copper(II) sulfate (displacement reaction)

1   Measure 50 cm^3 of copper(II) sulfate solution in the measuring cylinder and add the solution to the beaker.

2   Place one of the zinc strips in the beaker and leave it for five minutes.

3   Compare the colour of the zinc that was submerged in the copper(II) sulfate solution with the colour of the zinc that was not submerged in the copper(II) sulfate solution.

4   Record your observations in the table in the Recording data section.

Sodium chloride solution and silver nitrate (precipitation reaction)

1   Measure 15 cm^3 of sodium chloride solution in the measuring cylinder and add the solution to the test-tube.

2   Use a pipette to add 3 cm^3 of silver nitrate solution to the test-tube.

3   Record your observations in the table in the Recording data section.

Copper(II) carbonate (thermal decomposition)

1   Add a heaped spatula of copper(II) carbonate to the test-tube.

2   Set up the Bunsen burner on the heat-resistant mat.

3   Use the tongs to hold the test-tube in a blue flame and heat the test-tube for 30 seconds.

4   Record your observations in the table in the Recording data section.

Recording data

1 Record your observations in the table.

Reaction	Observations
Leaf discs/aquatic plant (*Elodea*)	
Burning magnesium	
Zinc and copper(II) sulfate	
Sodium chloride and silver nitrate	
Copper(II) carbonate	

> **TIP**
>
> A chemical change results in the formation of a new substance; a physical change does not change the chemical composition of a substance.

Analysis

2 For each of the reactions in the investigation where there were signs that a reaction was happening, decide what evidence there was for a chemical reaction.

    a   Leaf discs/aquatic plant (*Elodea*)

    ....

    ....

    b   Burning magnesium

    ....

    ....

    c   Zinc and copper(II) sulfate

    ....

    ....

    d   Sodium chloride and silver nitrate solution

    ....

    ....

e Copper(II) carbonate

....

....

....

Evaluation

3 Why was sodium hydrogen carbonate added to the solution before the leaf discs/aquatic plant were added?

....

....

4 Describe a control experiment for the aquatic plant investigation that would show that light is needed for photosynthesis.

....

....

5 Predict what gas was produced when copper(II) carbonate was heated. Research how you could test for this gas.

....

....

REFLECTION

A mind map is a way to organise concepts and the links between the ideas. It is a good way to visualise a whole topic. In the space provided, draw a mind map to show the signs you would look for to demonstrate that a chemical reaction had taken place.

Did you find it easy or difficult to draw the mind map?

Do you think this technique helps your learning and could you apply the technique to other topics?

Practical investigation 7.2: Endothermic and exothermic reactions

KEY WORDS

endothermic changes: a process or chemical reaction that takes in heat from the surroundings.
ΔH for an endothermic change has a positive value.

exothermic changes: a process or chemical reaction in which heat energy is produced and released to the surroundings.
ΔH for an exothermic change has a negative value.

IN THIS INVESTIGATION YOU WILL:

- learn that an exothermic reaction transfers thermal energy to its surroundings, leading to an increase in the temperature of the surroundings

- learn that an endothermic reaction takes in thermal energy from its surroundings, leading to a decrease in the temperature of the surroundings

- make careful measurements to obtain quantitative data on energy changes.

YOU WILL NEED:

- insulated cup and lid with a hole in the lid • beaker (250 cm³) • thermometer
- measuring cylinder (10 cm³) • spatula • copper(II) sulfate solution (0.4 mol/dm³)
- dilute hydrochloric acid (0.4 mol/dm³) • sodium hydrogen carbonate solution (0.4 mol/dm³)
- dilute sodium hydroxide (0.4 mol/dm³) • dilute citric acid (0.4 mol/dm³)
- magnesium powder • sodium carbonate • dilute ethanoic acid (0.05 mol/dm³)
- safety glasses • lab coat • gloves.

Safety

- Copper(II) sulfate is a moderate hazard and harmful to the aquatic environment. Waste from experiments using copper(II) sulfate solution must not be poured down the drain.

- Sodium hydroxide, sodium carbonate, citric acid and ethanoic acid are irritants.

- Hydrochloric acid is a moderate hazard.

- Magnesium powder is flammable.

- Wear eye protection throughout.

Getting started

You will be using an insulated cup with a lid in this experiment. Think about a possible reason for using an insulated cup instead of just using a glass beaker.

Method

1   Place the insulated cup in the 250 cm³ beaker. The beaker will help to keep the cup upright during the experiment.

2   Measure 10 cm³ of sodium hydrogen carbonate solution and add the solution to the insulated cup. Place the lid on the cup and insert the thermometer through the hole (Figure 7.1). Use the thermometer to measure the temperature and record the temperature in your results table. (You will need to design your data collection table in the Recording data section.)

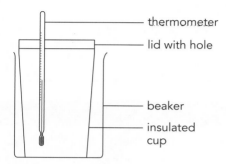

thermometer

lid with hole

beaker

insulated cup

Figure 7.1: Setup for measuring temperature changes in reactions.

3   Add four spatulas of citric acid to the cup and cover with the lid immediately. Use the thermometer to gently stir the mixture. Record the maximum or minimum temperature achieved.

> **TIP**
>
> Be careful not to remove the thermometer from the solution when taking a reading as this will affect your results.

4   Pour the mixture away and rinse the cup with water. Also rinse the thermometer with water.

5   Measure 10 cm³ of sodium hydroxide solution and add the solution to the insulated cup. Record the temperature as in step 2.

6   Add 10 cm³ of hydrochloric acid to the cup and cover with the lid. Use the thermometer to gently stir the mixture. Record the maximum or minimum temperature achieved.

7   Repeat step 4.

8   Measure 10 cm³ of copper(II) sulfate solution and add the solution to the insulated cup. Record the temperature as in step 2.

9   Add a spatula of magnesium powder to the cup and cover with the lid. Use the thermometer to gently stir the mixture. Record the maximum or minimum temperature achieved.

10 Repeat step 4.

11 Measure 10 cm³ of ethanoic acid and add the acid to the insulated cup. Record the temperature as in step 2.

12 Add a spatula of sodium carbonate to the cup and cover with the lid. Use the thermometer to gently stir the mixture. Record the maximum or minimum temperature achieved.

Recording data

1   In the space provided below, design a results table. Consider how many columns you will need as you will be recording the starting temperature and the maximum/minimum temperature.

Handling data

2   Calculate the temperature change for each of the reactions.

TIP

Remember to include a plus (+) or minus (−) sign in front of the temperature to show whether there was an increase or decrease in the temperature.

Reaction	Temperature change / °C
Sodium hydrogen carbonate and citric acid	
Sodium hydroxide and hydrochloric acid	
Copper(II) sulfate and magnesium powder	
Ethanoic acid and sodium carbonate	

Analysis

3   Which reactions were exothermic reactions and which were endothermic reactions?

a   The exothermic reactions were:

....

....

b The endothermic reactions were:

....

....

Evaluation

4 Look back at the Getting started section. Was your reason for using the insulated cup correct? If not, having now completed the investigation why do you think it was used?

....

....

5 How would the results have been affected by not using a lid on the cup?

....

....

6 If the solutions were left for a longer period of time, all of the solutions would return to the original temperature. Where does the heat energy go?

....

....

7 Why was it necessary to stir the solutions?

....

....

8 How could you improve this investigation to get more accurate results?

....

....

EXAM-STYLE QUESTIONS

1 Two students carried out an investigation to measure the temperature change when they mixed two solutions. This was their method:

Add $20\,cm^3$ of solution **A** to an insulated cup.

Use a thermometer to record the temperature of solution **A**.

Add $5\,cm^3$ of solution **B** and record the highest temperature reached.

Repeat the experiment using the same volume of solution **A** each time, but increasing the volume of **B** used by $5\,cm^3$ each time.

CONTINUED

a   Their results are given in the table below. The starting temperature for each solution was 25 °C. Record the temperatures shown in the thermometer diagrams in the table.

Volume of solution B added /	Thermometer diagram	Highest temperature reached / ......
5		
10		
15		
20		
25		
30		
35		

[7]

CONTINUED

b The units are missing from the table. Add the units to the table. **[2]**

c **Suggest** what volume of solution **B** could have been used as a control.

.... **[1]**

d Suggest why the students used an insulated cup.

.... **[1]**

e Construct a graph to show the results.

[5]

f The students each wrote a conclusion for the investigation. Read both of the conclusions. Tick the box for the conclusion you think is correct. **[1]**

Conclusion 1: This was an exothermic reaction as the temperature increased when the two solutions were mixed. ☐

Conclusion 2: This was an endothermic reaction as the temperature decreased when the two solutions were mixed. ☐

g Suggest how this investigation could have been improved to prevent heat being lost to the surroundings. **[1]**

[Total: 18]

> **COMMAND WORD**
>
> **suggest:** apply knowledge and understanding to situations where there are a range of valid responses in order to make proposals/ put forward considerations

CONTINUED

2   Plaster of Paris is often used to make casts of imprints found at crime scenes.
    When water is added to the dry powder, a reaction takes place. Some students
    want to investigate whether this reaction is exothermic or endothermic.
    Describe an investigation that the students could perform that would help
    them draw a conclusion about the type of reaction.

    ....

    ....

    ....

    ....

    .... [6]

COMMAND WORD

describe: state the
points of a topic /
give characteristics
and main features

3   When it is heated, copper(II) carbonate decomposes into copper oxide and
    carbon dioxide. Limewater can be used to test for the presence of carbon
    dioxide. The experimental setup is shown in the figure below.

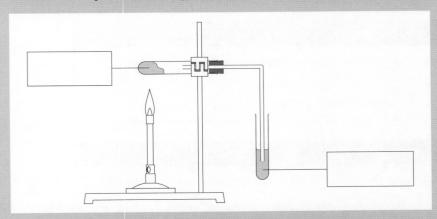

a   Add a label to one of the boxes to indicate the copper(II) carbonate.   [1]

b   Add a label to one of the boxes to indicate the limewater.   [1]

c   What type of flame would you use to heat the copper(II) carbonate?

    .... [1]

d   How could you tell when the copper(II) carbonate was completely
    decomposed to copper oxide?

    .... [1]

[Total: 4]

Chapter 8

Rate of reaction

THE INVESTIGATIONS IN THIS CHAPTER WILL:

- identify variables that affect the rate of reaction: temperature, surface area, concentration of solutions and the presence of a catalyst

- explore the use of catalysts to increase the rate of reaction

- use a variety of techniques to measure the rate of reaction

- enable you to interpret data from rate of reaction experiments.

Practical investigation 8.1:
The effect of temperature on reaction rate

KEY WORDS

catalyst: a substance that increases the rate of a chemical reaction but itself remains unchanged at the end of the reaction

reaction rate: a measure of how fast a reaction takes place

IN THIS INVESTIGATION YOU WILL:

- investigate how temperature affects the rate of reaction by measuring the volume of product in a given time

- use a gas syringe to measure gas volume

- describe the effects of increased temperature on the rate of reaction.

YOU WILL NEED:

- magnesium ribbon • dilute hydrochloric acid (0.5 mol/dm³) • conical flask (250 cm³)
- measuring cylinder (100 cm³) • stopper and delivery tube • gas syringe
- water-bath/kettle • ice • beaker (250 cm³) • boiling tube • thermometer
- clamp stand • timer • safety glasses • lab coat • gloves.

Safety

- As you will be using hot liquids, you must stand while completing the investigation.
- Report any spills to your teacher immediately.
- Hydrochloric acid is a moderate hazard.
- Wear eye protection throughout.

Getting started

Examine the gas syringe. Practise reading volumes from the scale. Discuss with your partner the reasons for choosing a gas syringe to measure the volume of gas produced.

Method

1   Set up the equipment to measure the volume of gas produced as shown in Figure 8.1.

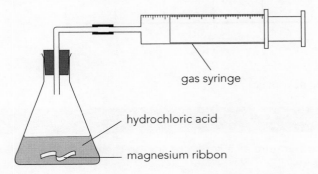

gas syringe

hydrochloric acid

magnesium ribbon

Figure 8.1: Setup for measuring the gas produced by magnesium reacting with hydrochloric acid.

2   Measure 25 cm³ of hydrochloric acid using the measuring cylinder and pour the hydrochloric acid into a boiling tube.

3   Prepare a water-bath for the boiling tube. This can be done by adding ice/boiling water to the 250 cm³ beaker. Measure the temperature using the thermometer. You need to use the following approximate temperatures: 0 °C, 10 °C, 15 °C and 30 °C. Remember to add the actual temperature you used to your results table. Place the boiling tube of hydrochloric acid in the beaker until the tube has reached the required temperature.

> **TIP**
>
> It will take about 15 seconds for the thermometer to record changes in temperature so add the ice or boiling water slowly and then wait to observe the temperature change.

4   Pour the hydrochloric acid into the conical flask and quickly add 3 cm of magnesium ribbon. Place the stopper connected to the delivery tube and gas syringe on to the conical flask immediately. Start the timer.

5   Record the volume of gas produced every minute in the results table in the Recording data section.

6 Once you have completed all of the data for the first temperature, dispose of the acid and repeat the experiment with the next temperature. Do not forget to reset the gas syringe.

Recording data

1 Record your data in the table below.

Temperature /°C	Volume of gas produced / cm³					
	0 min	1 min	2 min	3 min	4 min	5 min
	0					
	0					
	0					
	0					

Handling data

2 Plot a graph of your results on the next page.

TIP
You will need to show each temperature as a separate line on the graph and label each line with the temperature used.

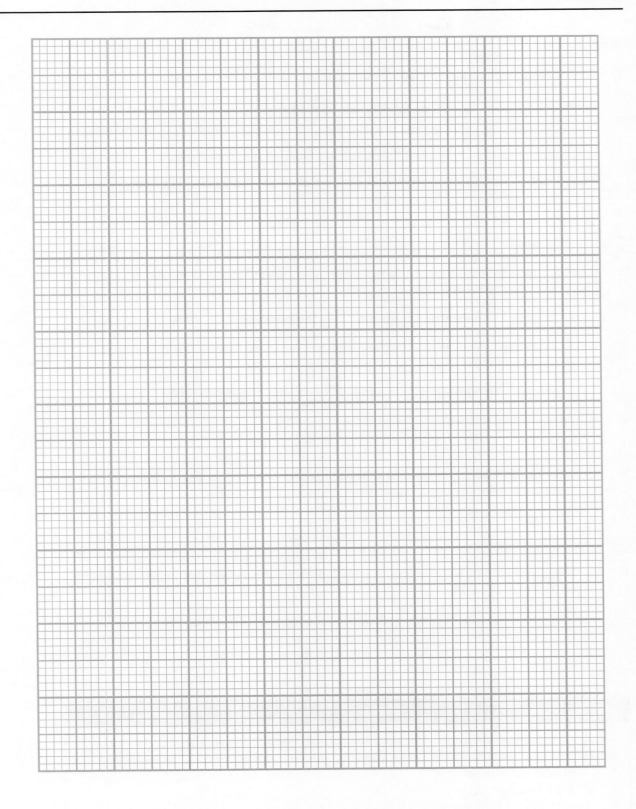

Analysis

3   Look at your graph and use the information to complete the following passage.

As the temperature of the acid is increased, the rate of reaction ....

The temperature with the fastest rate of reaction was ....°C. The temperature with the slowest

rate of reaction was ....°C. At 30°C the reaction occurred at its fastest at the start where the

line was the .... When the line levelled off, this demonstrated that the reaction

was ....

Evaluation

4   What was the independent variable in this experiment – which variable were you able to change? Circle the correct answer.

concentration of acid   temperature   time

5   What was the dependent variable in this experiment – which variable were you measuring? Circle the correct answer.

temperature   time   volume of gas produced

6   List three variables that were controlled in this experiment.

....

7   If the experiment was repeated with acid heated to 60°C, how long do you think it would take for the reaction to finish? Give a reason for your answer.

....

....

8   Can you identify two possible sources of error and suggest what effect they might have had on the results obtained?

....

....

....

REFLECTION

As part of the reflection for this investigation you will need to ask your partner to assess your graph; you will also assess theirs. The criteria for assessing the graph is as follows:
*   Axes labelled with units
*   Points plotted accurately
*   Smooth line of best fit for each line
*   Each line labelled with temperature.

Practical investigation 8.2:
The effect of catalysts on rate of reaction

IN THIS INVESTIGATION YOU WILL:

- use a variety of catalysts with the aim of finding which catalyst increases the rate of reaction the most

- determine reaction times for different catalysts

- explain the effect of catalysts on the rate of reaction.

YOU WILL NEED:

- timer • two glass measuring cylinders ($25\,cm^3$) • dropping pipette
- piece of paper • black marker pen • conical flask ($250\,cm^3$)
- samples of catalysts (copper(II) sulfate solution ($0.1\,mol/dm^3$), iron(II) sulfate solution ($0.1\,mol/dm^3$)) • $100\,cm^3$ sodium thiosulfate solution ($0.1\,mol/dm^3$)
- $100\,cm^3$ iron(III) nitrate solution ($0.1\,mol/dm^3$) • safety glasses • lab coat • gloves.

Safety

- All solutions are moderate hazards.
- Copper(II) sulfate is a moderate hazard and harmful to the aquatic environment. Waste from experiments using copper(II) sulfate must not be poured down the drain.

Getting started

You will need to measure liquids accurately in this investigation. Practise measuring the following volumes of water in the measuring cylinder: $5\,cm^3$, $10\,cm^3$, $15\,cm^3$ and $25\,cm^3$.

TIP

A graduated dropping pipette can be used to add small volumes of liquid to a beaker or flask.

Method

1   Using the black marker pen, draw a thick black cross ('X') on the paper. Place the paper with the cross under the conical flask. Measure $25\,cm^3$ of sodium thiosulfate solution using one of the measuring cylinders. Add the sodium thiosulfate solution to the conical flask.

2   Look down on the conical flask from above. The black cross should be clearly visible (Figure 8.2).

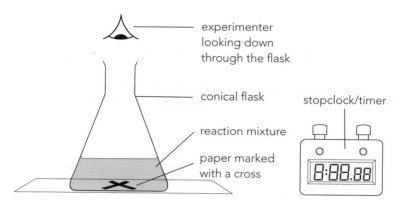

Figure 8.2: Observing a black cross through a solution.

3   Measure 25 cm³ of iron(III) nitrate solution using the other measuring cylinder.

4   Prepare the timer and then pour the iron(III) nitrate solution into the conical flask. Start the timer.

5   The solution should initially become opaque (cloudy) and the cross should disappear. Stop the timer when the cross can be seen again. Record the time taken for the cross to become visible in your results table. (You will need to design your data collection table in the Recording data section.)

6   Pour away the sodium thiosulfate and iron(III) nitrate mixture. Rinse out the conical flask.

7   Repeat steps 2–6, but this time use the dropping pipette to add a single drop of one of the catalysts to the iron(III) nitrate when it is still in the measuring cylinder.

8   Repeat the experiment for each catalyst and record the data obtained in your results table.

Recording data

1   Design a table to show the time taken for the cross to disappear (reaction time) for each of the catalysts and for when no catalyst was used.

Handling data

2   Draw a bar chart to show your results.

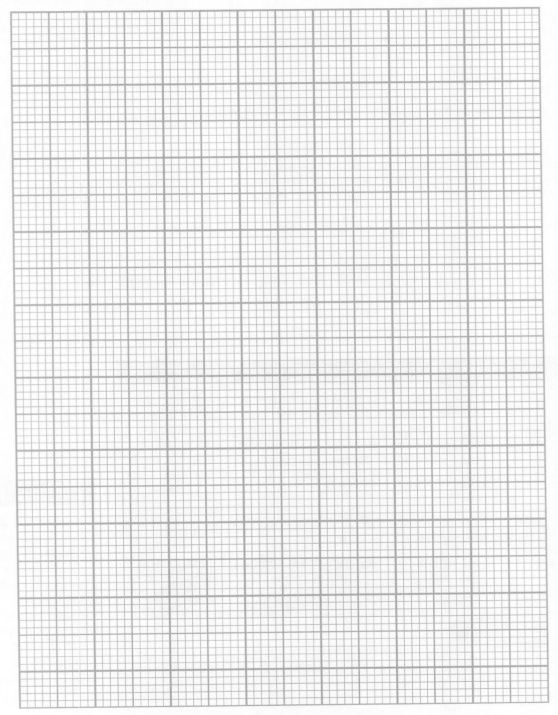

Analysis

3   List the catalysts in order from the most effective to the least effective.

....

....

Evaluation

4   Why was only one drop of each catalyst used in this investigation?

....

5   Some of the catalysts used in this investigation caused the solution to become clear very quickly. How could the reaction have been slowed down? (Think about which other variables affect the rate of reaction.)

....

....

6   Can you suggest a more accurate method for determining when the reaction was finished?

....

EXAM-STYLE QUESTIONS

1   A student was investigating the effect of surface area on the rate of reaction. He had three samples of calcium carbonate: powder, small lumps and one large lump. Calcium carbonate reacts with sulfuric acid to produce carbon dioxide gas. He measured the volume of gas produced each minute for five minutes using a gas syringe for each of the three samples.

a   How could the student test that the gas produced was carbon dioxide?   [1]

b   **Suggest** two control variables for this experiment.   [2]

c   Complete the table below for sulfuric acid.   [3]

Test		
	Methyl orange	Blue litmus paper	Universal indicator
Colour			

COMMAND WORD

suggest: apply knowledge and understanding to situations where there are a range of valid responses in order to make proposals/ put forward considerations

CONTINUED

The results of the investigation are given in the table below.

Time /	Calcium carbonate powder: volume of gas produced /	Calcium carbonate small lumps: volume of gas produced /	Calcium carbonate large lump: volume of gas produced / ....
0	0	0	0
1	18	9	3
2	25	15	5
3	25	19	6
4	25	23	7
5	25	25	8

d   Add in the missing units to the column headings.   [2]

e   Plot a graph to show the results.

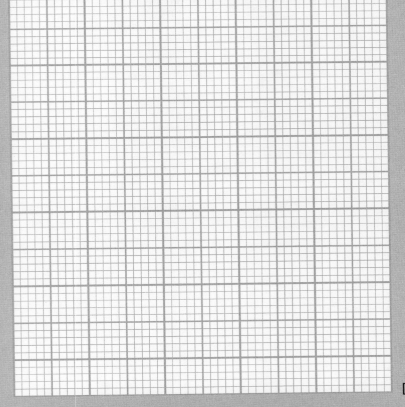

[5]

CONTINUED

f Suggest how many minutes it took for all of the powdered calcium carbonate to react and give a reason for your answer.

....

.... [2]

g The student also had a sample of very finely ground calcium carbonate powder. Use the information from the table and your graph to predict how long it would take for this powder to completely react with the acid.

.... [1]

[Total: 16]

2 Hydrogen peroxide decomposes to form oxygen and water. The reaction can be summarised using the following symbol equation:

$$2H_2O_2\ (.........) \rightarrow 2H_2O\ (.........) + O_2\ (.........)$$

a Add the state symbols to the symbol equation above. [3]

This reaction happens very slowly. It is possible to increase the rate of this reaction by adding a catalyst.

b Design an experiment to compare the three catalysts, iron(III) oxide, manganese(IV) oxide and lead(IV) oxide, to see which catalyst has the greatest effect on the rate of reaction.

....

....

....

....

....

.... [5]

[Total: 8]

Chapter 9

Reversible reactions and equilibrium

THE INVESTIGATIONS IN THIS CHAPTER WILL:

- explore both forwards favouring reactions (the formation of the products) and backwards favouring reactions (the formation of the reactants)

- show that, depending on the conditions present, reactions can favour the forwards or backwards direction

- demonstrate a laboratory version of the industrial process for making fertiliser.

Practical investigation 9.1: Reversible reactions

KEY WORDS

dynamic (chemical) equilibrium: two chemical reactions, one the reverse of the other, taking place at the same time, where the concentrations of the reactants and products remain constant because the rate at which the forward reaction occurs is the same as that of the reverse reaction

hydrated salts: salts whose crystals contain combined water (*water of crystallisation*) as part of the structure

reversible reaction: a chemical reaction that can go either forwards or backwards, depending on the conditions

IN THIS INVESTIGATION YOU WILL:

- show that some chemical reactions can be reversed by observing changes in appearance

- learn that changing the conditions can change the direction of a reversible reaction.

YOU WILL NEED:

Copper ions equilibrium:

- test-tube rack   • three test-tubes   • two pipettes
- copper(II) sulfate solution (1.0 mol/dm³)   • ammonia solution (1.0 mol/dm³)
- dilute sulfuric acid solution (1.0 mol/dm³)   • measuring cylinder (10 cm³)
- permanent marker pen   • safety glasses   • lab coat   • gloves.

Carbon dioxide and water:

- sodium hydroxide solution (0.4 mol/dm³)   • conical flask (250 cm³)   • phenol red indicator solution   • distilled water   • measuring cylinder (100 cm³)   • tripod
- gauze   • spatula   • Bunsen burner   • heat-resistant mat   • safety glasses
- lab coat   • gloves.

Hydrated copper(II) sulfate:

- powdered copper(II) sulfate   • evaporating basin   • tripod   • gauze   • spatula
- Bunsen burner   • heat-resistant mat   • distilled water   • safety glasses
- lab coat   • gloves.

Safety

- Sulfuric acid is a moderate hazard.

- Sodium hydroxide and ammonia solution are irritants.

- Copper(II) sulfate is a moderate hazard and harmful to the aquatic environment. Waste from experiments using copper(II) sulfate must not be poured down the drain.

- Phenol red indicator is highly flammable, so keep the phenol red away from any naked flames.

- Allow the evaporating basin to cool and take care when adding water to the basin.

- Wear eye protection throughout.

Getting started

Collect a pipette. Practise accurately measuring different volumes of water. Try to measure the following volumes: 0.5 cm³, 1.5 cm³, 2.5 cm³ and 3 cm³. Once you are confident at measuring volumes, practise using the pipette to deliver one drop of water at a time. This takes skill but is very important in this investigation.

TIP

It is difficult to collect the exact volume of liquid you want in a pipette. An easier method is to collect more liquid than needed and then remove the extra liquid by gently squeezing the pipette bulb.

Method

The investigations can be performed in any order.

Copper ions equilibrium

1   Label the tubes 1, 2 and 3 with the marker pen. Place the three test-tubes in the test-tube rack and add 1 cm³ of copper(II) sulfate to the first two tubes.

2   Use the pipette to add ammonia solution drop-wise to the first tube until you see a colour change. Be sure to shake the tube gently after each drop is added. Record the colour change in the results table in the Recording data section. Pour half of the mixture into tube 2 and half of the mixture into tube 3.

3   Continue to add ammonia solution one drop at a time to tube 2 until you see another colour change.

4   Add dilute sulfuric acid one drop at a time to the tube 3. Remember to shake the tube after adding each drop. Stop adding the acid when you observe a colour change. Record your observations.

Carbon dioxide and water

1   Pour 100 cm³ of distilled water into the conical flask.

2   Add two drops of phenol red indicator to the water.

3   Add drops of sodium hydroxide to the solution until the solution changes colour. Record the colour in the results table in the Recording data section.

4   Breathe into the flask until the solution changes colour.

5   Set up the tripod, gauze, heat-resistant mat and Bunsen burner.

6   Gently heat the conical flask until the colour changes. (Do not boil the solution.)

Hydrated copper(II) sulfate

1   Add four spatulas of copper(II) sulfate to the evaporating dish.

2   Set up the tripod, gauze, heat-resistant mat and Bunsen burner. Place the evaporating basin on the gauze and heat the basin gently on a blue flame.

3   Stop heating the evaporating basin when the copper(II) sulfate changes colour.

4   Allow the evaporating basin to cool back to room temperature for about five minutes. You could use this time to pack away the rest of the apparatus or begin one of the other experiments.

5   Add a few drops of distilled water. Record the colour change in the results table in the Recording data section.

> **TIP**
>
> Distilled water is purified water without any contaminants or minerals.

Recording data

> **1**   Record the observations to your investigations in the tables below.

Copper ions equilibrium

Tube	Colour changes
1	
2	
3	

Carbon dioxide and water

	Colour observed
Sodium hydroxide added	
Air exhaled into the flask	
Flask heated	

Hydrated copper(II) sulfate

	Colour observed
After heating	
After adding water	

Analysis

> **2**   What type of reaction is occurring between the ammonia solution and the sulfuric acid in the copper ions equilibrium reaction?
>
> ....
>
> **3**   Why was sodium hydroxide added to the conical flask in the carbon dioxide and water investigations?
>
> ....
>
> **4**   Why did heating the conical flask return the solution to an alkaline pH as indicated by the change to red?
>
> ....

5   Write the word equation for the reaction that took place when hydrated copper(II) sulfate was heated.

....

Evaluation

6   Use what you have learnt in the investigation to design an experiment to collect the water that was given off by the hydrated copper(II) sulfate when it was heated.

....

....

....

....

....

....

....

TIP

Always design experiments as a series of numbered steps.

REFLECTION

The design of experiments is very important. Think about previous practicals you have performed. Did the methods used in the other practicals help you to design the experiment here?

What factors do all experiments have in common? Think about how you could apply your knowledge of these factors to the planning of new experiments.

Practical investigation 9.2: Making ammonium sulfate – a plant fertiliser

KEY WORDS

fertiliser: a substance added to the soil to replace essential elements lost when crops are harvested, which enables crops to grow faster and increases the yield

neutralisation: a chemical reaction between an acid and a base to produce a salt and water only; summarised by the ionic equation $H^+(aq) + OH^-(aq) \rightarrow H_2O(l)$

IN THIS INVESTIGATION YOU WILL:

- use a laboratory version of the industrial process for making an artificial fertiliser

- use neutralisation as an indicator that a reaction has taken place

- use separation techniques to collect a final product.

TIP

Ammonium salts are used as fertilisers to provide nitrogen for improved plant growth.

YOU WILL NEED:

- measuring cylinder ($25\,cm^3$) • ammonia solution ($2.0\,mol/dm^3$)
- sulfuric acid ($1.0\,mol/dm^3$) • universal indicator paper • glass rod
- heat resistant mat • Bunsen burner • tripod • gauze • pipette
- beaker ($50\,cm^3$) • evaporating dish • safety glasses • lab coat • gloves.

Safety

- Ammonia solution is corrosive. When ammonia solution is heated it may give off ammonia gas, which is harmful if inhaled.

- Sulfuric acid is a moderate hazard.

- Wear eye protection throughout.

Getting started

You will be using a glass rod in this investigation. Practise collecting a small amount of water on the end of the glass rod and transferring the liquid onto a piece of paper.

Method

1   Use the measuring cylinder to measure $25\,cm^3$ of the ammonia solution. Pour the ammonia solution into the evaporating basin.

2   Pour the sulfuric acid into the beaker until it is two-thirds full.

3   Using the pipette add $1\,cm^3$ of sulfuric acid to the evaporating dish.

4   Dip the glass rod into the solution in the evaporating dish and then dab the end of the glass rod onto a piece of universal indicator paper. The paper should turn blue/violet.

5   Repeats steps 3 and 4, using a fresh piece of universal indicator paper each time until the ammonia solution has been neutralised by the sulfuric acid (universal indictor paper changes colour to green). Record the volume of sulfuric acid that you used in the results table in the recording data section.

6   Place the Bunsen burner on the heat-resistant mat. Set up the tripod with the gauze on top.
     Place the evaporating dish on top of the gauze as shown in Figure 9.1.

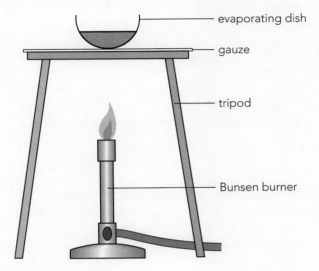

Figure 9.1: Setup for making ammonium sulfate.

7   Light the Bunsen burner and heat the evaporating dish on a cool blue flame until most of the
     solution has evaporated away. If the solution is boiling too vigorously, remove the Bunsen
     burner from under the evaporating dish.

TIP
Do not heat the evaporating dish to complete dryness.

8   Turn off the Bunsen burner and allow the evaporating dish to cool.

9   Small crystals should be visible around the edges of the evaporating dish.

Recording data

1   Record your results in the results table. If possible collect the results from other groups as well
     or repeat the experiment more than once. Add the units to the results table.

Volume of sulfuric acid added / .... 1st trial/group	Volume of sulfuric acid added /.......... 2nd trial/group	Volume of sulfuric acid added /.......... 3rd trial/group

Handling data

2   If you collected other group data or completed repeat trials, calculate the mean volume of sulfuric acid used to neutralise the ammonia solution.

Mean volume of sulfuric acid added: ....

Analysis

3   Write the word equation for the reaction taking place between ammonia solution and sulfuric acid.

....

4   Write the balanced symbol equation for the reaction, including state symbols.
Ammonia solution = NH_4OH, sulfuric acid = H_2SO_4, ammonium sulfate = $(NH_4)_2SO_4$

....

Evaluation

5   How could you have obtained more precise data for the volume of sulfuric acid needed to neutralise the ammonia solution?

....

....

6   Why was universal indicator not added to the ammonia solution?

....

7   Suggest an alternative way that the pH of the solutions in this investigation could have been measured.

....

8   Design an improved version of this investigation to obtain more precise and reliable data for the volume of sulfuric acid needed to neutralise the ammonia solution.

....

....

....

....

....

....

EXAM-STYLE QUESTIONS

1 A student wants to demonstrate that copper(II) sulfate can be dehydrated and rehydrated in a reversible reaction. **Suggest** a method he could use to demonstrate this property.

....

....

....

....

.... [6]

2 Two students were investigating hydrated copper(II) sulfate crystals. They set up the apparatus shown in the diagram below.

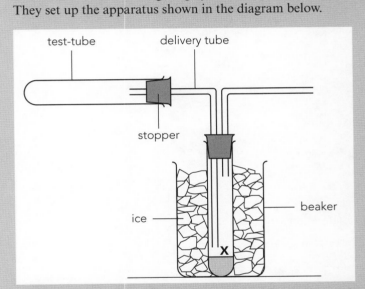

The students want to dehydrate the copper(II) sulfate crystals.

a **Sketch**, on the diagram, where the copper(II) sulfate crystals should be placed. [1]

b On the diagram, add an arrow to indicate where heat should be applied. [1]

c Why is it important that the glass delivery tube is not submerged in water at point X on the diagram?

....

.... [1]

d Why is ice placed around the test-tube?

.... [1]

COMMAND WORDS

suggest: apply knowledge and understanding to situations where there are a range of valid responses in order to make proposals/ put forward considerations

sketch: make a simple freehand drawing showing the key features, taking care over proportions

CONTINUED

e What colour would you expect the copper(II) sulfate crystals to be after the crystals were heated?

.... [1]

[Total: 5]

3 Copper(II) sulfate can be used to increase the copper content of soil. Two students are making copper(II) sulfate crystals to be used as a plant fertiliser. To prepare the salt they must first add excess copper oxide with $25\,cm^3$ of warm sulfuric acid.

a Suggest a suitable piece of apparatus for each of the following procedures:

   i To measure the volume of sulfuric acid needed

   .... [1]

   ii To add the copper oxide to the sulfuric acid

   .... [1]

   iii To stir the mixture

   .... [1]

   iv To heat the beaker containing the mixture

   .... [1]

b What does the word 'excess' mean?

.... [1]

c Suggest a method for obtaining the copper(II) sulfate from the solution formed.

....

....

....

.... [5]

[Total: 10]

> Chapter 10

Redox reactions

THE INVESTIGATIONS IN THIS CHAPTER WILL:

- enable you to identify reactions as oxidation or reduction reactions

- produce evidence of redox reactions by observations and data collected by measuring temperature changes

- enable you to identify oxidising and reducing agents by observing different reactions.

Practical investigation 10.1: Energy changes during redox reactions

KEY WORDS

oxidation: there are three definitions of oxidation:
i   a reaction in which oxygen is added to an element or compound
ii   a reaction involving the loss of electrons from an atom, molecule or ion
iii a reaction in which the oxidation state of an element is increased

redox reaction: a reaction involving both reduction and oxidation

reduction: there are three definitions of reduction:
i   a reaction in which oxygen is removed from a compound
ii   a reaction involving the gain of electrons by an atom, molecule or ion
iii a reaction in which the oxidation state of an element is decreased

IN THIS INVESTIGATION YOU WILL:

- complete a series of redox reactions using a variety of metals and a metal salt in solution

- accurately measure temperature changes and volumes of solutions

- identify which reactants are being oxidised and which reactants are being reduced in a redox reaction.

YOU WILL NEED:

- insulated cup and a lid with a hole • beaker ($250\,cm^3$) • thermometer
- measuring cylinder ($25\,cm^3$ or $50\,cm^3$) • copper(II) sulfate solution ($1.0\,mol/dm^3$)
- spatula • clamp stand and clamp • glass rod • zinc powder • iron filings
- magnesium powder • copper powder • safety glasses • lab coat • gloves.

Safety

- Magnesium powder is flammable.
- All of the powdered metals except for copper are flammable.
- Copper(II) sulfate is a moderate hazard and harmful to the aquatic environment. Waste from experiments using copper(II) sulfate must not be poured down the drain.
- Wear eye protection throughout.

Getting started

Look at the equipment list. You may have used these pieces of apparatus in previous practicals. Make sure you understand the reason why each piece of apparatus is used. For example:

Why is the insulated cup with a lid used?

....

....

Why is the beaker included in the equipment list?

....

....

Method

1   Place the insulated cup inside the beaker. Attach the thermometer to the clamp on the stand so that you are able to lower the thermometer into the insulated cup through the hole in the lid (see Figure 10.1).

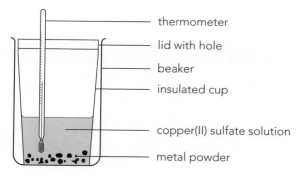

thermometer

lid with hole

beaker

insulated cup

copper(II) sulfate solution

metal powder

Figure 10.1: Setup to measure temperature changes in displacement reactions.

2   Measure 25 cm³ of copper(II) sulfate and pour it into the cup. Lower the thermometer into the cup and record the starting temperature.

3   Remove the lid and thermometer. Add one spatula of iron filings to the cup and stir the mixture with the glass rod. Replace the lid and thermometer, and record the highest temperature reached in your table in the Recording data section. (This may take a few minutes.)

4   Remove the lid and thermometer and pour away the mixture following your teacher's instructions. Rinse the cup out with water. Repeat steps 1–3 with the magnesium, copper and zinc powder.

Recording data

1   Design a table to show your results. Remember you will need enough rows in your table for each type of metal. Add enough columns to record the starting temperature, highest temperature and the temperature change.

Handling data

2   Draw a graph to show the temperature change for each type of metal.

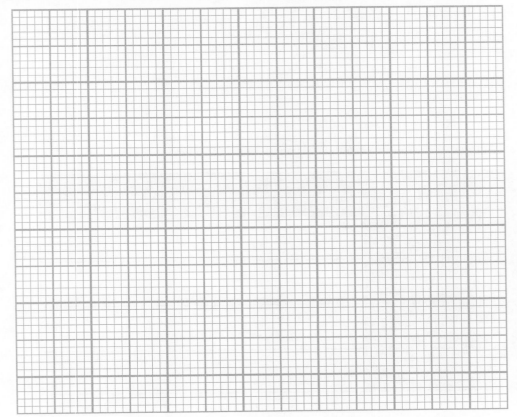

Analysis

3 What is a temperature change evidence for?

....

4 Which metal produced the biggest temperature change?

....

5 Which metal produced the smallest temperature change and why do you think this was?

....

6 Complete the word equations and write the symbol equations for each of the redox reactions:

Iron + copper(II) sulfate → .... + ...

.... + ... → .... + ...

Magnesium + copper(II) sulfate → .... + ...

.... + ... → .... + ...

Copper + copper(II) sulfate → .... + ...

.... + ... → .... + ...

Zinc + copper(II) sulfate → .... + ...

.... + ... → .... + ...

7 Look back at your answers for question **6** to help you fill in the table below.

Reaction	Element being oxidised	Element being reduced
iron + copper(II) sulfate		
magnesium + copper(II) sulfate		
copper + copper(II) sulfate		
zinc + copper(II) sulfate		

> **TIP**
>
> Oxidation is the gain of oxygen and reduction is the loss of oxygen. Redox reactions involve simultaneous reduction and oxidation.

Evaluation

8   Why did you have to measure the starting temperature of the copper(II) sulfate?

....

....

9   List the variables that you controlled in this investigation.

....

....

10   How could you have obtained more reliable data?

....

....

11   Name a variable that you did not control in this investigation.

....

12   What effect could this have had on your results?

....

....

Practical investigation 10.2: Identifying oxidising and reducing agents

IN THIS INVESTIGATION YOU WILL:

- identify which reactants are being oxidised and which reactants are being reduced in redox reactions by making careful observations

> learn how potassium iodide and acidified potassium manganate can be used to identify oxidising and reducing agents

> record colour changes in the tests for oxidising and reducing agents.

YOU WILL NEED:

- aqueous iron(III) sulfate (0.5 mol/dm³) • acidified potassium manganate (0.1 mol/dm³)
- pipettes • white spotting tile • potassium iodide (0.1 mol/dm³)
- potassium bromide • potassium chloride • copper(II) sulfate solution (0.5 mol/dm³)
- marker pen • starch solution • optional: beaker for used pipettes • safety glasses
- lab coat • gloves.

Safety

- Iron(III) sulfate is an irritant and a moderate hazard.

- Potassium manganate is an irritant, harmful if swallowed and can stain skin.

- Copper(II) sulfate is a moderate hazard and harmful to the aquatic environment. Waste from experiments using copper(II) sulfate must not be poured down the drain.

- Wash your hands after the investigation or wear gloves throughout.

- Wear eye protection throughout.

Getting started

The white spotting tile is useful when trying to observe colour changes. Practise using a pipette and adding 0.5 cm³ of water to the wells of the spotting tile.

Method

Identifying oxidising agents

1   Use the marker pen to label three wells on the spotting tiles 1, 2 and 3.

2   Use a pipette to add $0.5\,cm^3$ of copper(II) sulfate to each of the three wells on the spotting tile.

> **TIP**
>
> It is important to use clean pipettes each time you transfer a different liquid. Use a beaker to hold used pipettes to make sure that you do not reuse a pipette by mistake.

3   Using a clean pipette, add 3–4 drops of potassium chloride to well number 1.
    Record your observation of any colour change in the results table in the Recording data section.

4   Repeat step 3 for potassium bromide into well number 2 and potassium iodide in well number 3.

5   Shake the starch solution. Use a pipette to add 3–4 drops of starch solution to each of the three wells. Record any colour changes in the results table.

Identifying reducing agents

1   Using a pipette, add $2\,cm^3$ of acidified potassium manganate to an empty well on the spotting tile. Record the colour of the solution in the results table in the Recording data section.

2   Use a clean pipette to add iron(III) sulfate a few drops at a time until there is a colour change. Record the colour change in the results table.

Recording data

1   Write the colour changes observed into the results tables.

Oxidising agents

	Potassium chloride	Potassium bromide	Potassium iodide
Copper(II) sulfate			
Starch			

Reducing agents

	Acidified potassium manganate
Iron(III) sulfate	

Analysis

2 What conclusion can you draw from the result of the reaction between potassium chloride, potassium bromide and potassium iodide with copper(II) sulfate?

....

3 Starch reacts with iodine to produce a dark black precipitate. What conclusion can you draw from your observations of the colour change when starch was added to the potassium iodide and copper(II) sulfate solution?

....

....

4 Write the word equation for the reaction that took place between copper(II) sulfate and potassium iodide.

.... + ... → .... + ... +

....

5 From the word equation for question **4**, what was the element being oxidised and the element being reduced?

Oxidised: ....

Reduced: ....

6 Suggest why there was no colour change when potassium chloride was added to the copper(II) sulfate.

....

7 Acidified potassium manganate changes from purple to colourless in the presence of a reducing agent. What conclusion can you draw from the colour change you observed when iron(III) sulfate was added to the acidified potassium manganate?

....

....

Evaluation

8 Why was it necessary to use the starch solution?

....

REFLECTION

You have now learnt how to test for oxidising agents and reducing agents. In the space provided summarise what you have learnt. Ask your partner to evaluate your table. Do they agree that is a correct summary?

	Chemical test	Result
Oxidising agents		
Reducing agents		

Do you think summary tables are a useful way of remembering what you have learnt?

Think about how you could expand this summary table to include additional relevant information. What other techniques have you developed to help you remember important information?

EXAM-STYLE QUESTIONS

1 Two students were trying to identify some unknown liquids. The liquids were either oxidising or reducing agents.

    a   i   **Suggest** a chemical test for a reducing agent.

           .... [1]

        ii For the test you have chosen in part **i**, **state** the result you would expect to see if a reducing agent was present.

           .... [1]

    b   i   Suggest a chemical test for an oxidising agent.

           .... [1]

        ii For the test you have chosen in part **i**, state the result you would expect to see if an oxidising agent was present.

           .... [1]

                                                          [Total: 4]

COMMAND WORDS

suggest: apply knowledge and understanding to situations where there are a range of valid responses in order to make proposals/ put forward considerations

state: express in clear terms

CONTINUED

2   A student was investigating redox reactions. They added a strip of magnesium to a test-tube containing copper(II) sulfate solution.

   a   i   **Describe** how the appearance of the solution would change.

   .... [1]

   ii   Describe how the appearance of the magnesium would change.

   .... [1]

   b   i   What is the oxidation number of copper in copper(II) sulfate?

   .... [1]

   ii   **Define** the term *reduction*.

   .... [1]

   iii   Define the term *oxidation*.

   .... [1]

   c   Energy is given out during the reaction between copper(II) sulfate and magnesium.

   i   State the name for reactions that release energy to the surroundings.

   .... [1]

   ii   Suggest a simple piece of apparatus that could be used to measure the enthalpy change during the reaction between copper(II) sulfate and magnesium.

   .... [1]

   [Total: 7]

COMMAND WORDS

describe: state the points of a topic / give characteristics and main features

define: give precise meaning

Chapter 11

Acids and bases

THE INVESTIGATIONS IN THIS CHAPTER WILL:

- look at acids and bases and the differences between them

> explore both strong and weak acids and their interactions

- use different indicators to identify acids and alkalis

- enable you to evaluate acidity or alkalinity using the pH scale

- enable you to categorise metal oxides based on their pH.

Practical investigation 11.1: Weak and strong acids

KEY WORDS

acid: a substance that dissolves in water, producing $H^+(aq)$ ions – a solution of an acid turns litmus red and has a pH below 7.
Acids act as proton donors

alkalis: soluble bases that produce $OH^-(aq)$ ions in water – a solution of an alkali turns litmus blue and has a pH above 7

indicator: a substance that changes colour when added to acidic or alkaline solutions, e.g. litmus or thymolphthalein

methyl orange: an acid–base indicator that is red in acidic and yellow in alkaline solutions

pH scale: a scale running from below 0 to 14, used for expressing the acidity or alkalinity of a solution; a neutral solution has a pH of 7

universal indicator: a mixture of indicators that has different colours in solutions of different pH

IN THIS INVESTIGATION YOU WILL:

- use universal indicator to quantify the pH value of different acids

> evaluate the strength of acids by making a number of different observations

- identify the product produced when reacting acids with metal.

YOU WILL NEED:

- 10 cm³ of each of two acids X and Y • sodium hydroxide solution (0.4 mol/dm³)
- sodium carbonate solution (0.4 mol/dm³) • universal indicator solution
- universal indicator colour chart • one piece of blue litmus paper • methyl orange
- test-tubes • test-tube rack • four pipettes • spatula • two beakers (100 cm³)
- matches • splints • spotting tile • measuring cylinder (10 cm³) • gloves
- two pieces of magnesium ribbon • permanent marker • safety glasses • lab coat.

Safety

- Report any acid spills to your teacher immediately. Universal indicator will stain clothing and skin.

- Methyl orange indicator is corrosive, flammable, a health and moderate hazard, hazardous to the aquatic environment, and is acutely toxic.

- Sodium hydroxide and sodium carbonates are irritants.

- Wear eye protection throughout.

Getting started

Familiarise yourself with the pH scale for universal indicator. Make sure you know which end of the scale is acidic and which end of the scale is alkaline. Complete the table to show the correct colour for each of the different substances.

Substance	Universal indicator colour
Strongly acidic	
Weakly acidic	
Neutral	
Weakly alkaline	
Strongly alkaline	

Method

1   Using a pipette, add 2 cm³ of acid X into each of four test-tubes. Label these test-tubes with an X and place them in the test-tube rack. Repeat for acid Y with four fresh test-tubes.

2   Measure 10 cm³ of sodium carbonate solution and pour the solution into a beaker. Do the same for the sodium hydroxide solution using another beaker.

3   Add two drops of universal indicator to two of the tubes containing acid X. Repeat for acid Y. Record the colour change in the table in the Recording data section.

4   Using a clean pipette, slowly add drops of sodium carbonate solution to the first test-tube containing acid X and universal indicator. Count how many drops you have to add before the solution becomes neutral. You will need to shake the tube to get the solutions to mix properly. In the table, record the number of drops needed and also a description of the reaction. Repeat for acid Y.

5   In the next two test-tubes containing acids X and Y with universal indicator, repeat the procedure but this time use a clean pipette and the sodium hydroxide solution. In the table, record the number of drops and also a description of the reaction. Remember to shake the tubes to ensure adequate mixing.

6   Take a piece of magnesium ribbon and add it to the next test-tube containing acid X. Record a description of the reaction in the table. Collect the gas given off using an empty test-tube placed upside down over the reaction tube. After about 30 seconds, place a lighted splint over the mouth of the upside down test-tube (Figure 11.1). Record the result. Repeat for acid Y.

> **TIP**
>
> Hold your thumb over the mouth of the test-tube before testing the gas with a lighted splint as this will concentrate any gas and give a better result.

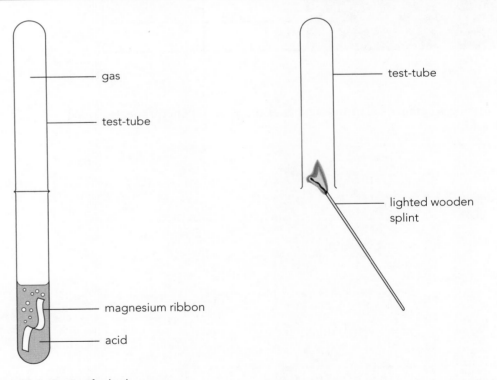

Figure 11.1: Testing for hydrogen gas.

7   Add three drops of methyl orange to each of two wells on your spotting tile. Rip a small piece of blue litmus paper and add a piece of the paper to each of two wells.

8 Using a pipette, take a small amount of acid X from the remaining tube labelled acid X and add a few drops to one methyl orange well and one litmus paper well. Repeat for acid Y.

Recording data

1 Record your results in the table.

Test	Acid X	Acid Y
Sodium carbonate – reaction		
Sodium carbonate – drops needed		
Sodium hydroxide – reaction		
Sodium hydroxide – drops needed		
Magnesium reaction		
Gas given off during magnesium reaction		
Blue litmus paper		
Methyl orange		
Universal indicator		

Handling data

2 Draw a bar chart to show a comparison of the number of drops of sodium carbonate needed to neutralise each acid.

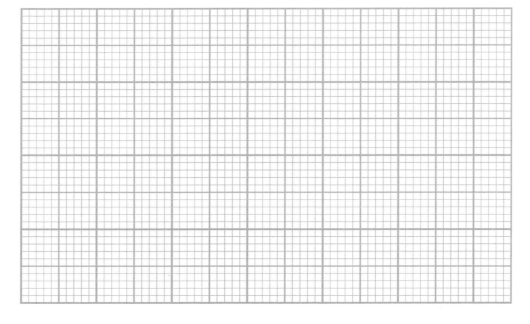

Analysis

3   Use the words below to complete the sentences.

alkalis   hydrogen   lighted   metal   more   neutralise

red   strength   stronger   vigorous   weaker

In this investigation, various tests were used to compare the .... of the two

acids. A strong acid would require .... drops of both sodium hydroxide and

sodium carbonate solution to .... the acid. A .... acid would

require fewer drops of the .... to neutralise the acid. The reaction between

strong acids and alkalis is more .... than between weak acids and alkalis.

Magnesium is a .... and so will react with an acid to produce

.... gas and there will be more effervescence produced in reaction with

a .... acid.

The test for hydrogen gas is a .... splint, which produces a squeaky pop.

Blue litmus paper and methyl orange turn .... in the presence of acid.

4   Use your results to complete these sentences.

Universal indicator changes .... depending on how acidic or alkaline

a solution is.

The colour change observed for acid X was .... and therefore the acid has

a pH of ....

The colour change observed for acid Y was .... and therefore the acid has

a pH of ....

Evaluation

5   Which of the tests were useful for determining the strength of each acid?

....

6   Which of the tests were not useful for determining the strength of each acid? Give a reason.

....

....

7   Suggest how many drops of sodium hydroxide would need to be added to an acid with a pH of 4 to neutralise the acid.

....

REFLECTION

Think about the many different steps involved in this investigation. Which parts did you find easy and which parts did you find difficult?

What could you do to help you perform these types of investigations?

....

....

Practical investigation 11.2: Investigating relative acidity

KEY WORD

base: a substance that neutralises an acid, producing a salt and water as the only products. Bases act as proton acceptors

IN THIS INVESTIGATION YOU WILL:

- use a variety of acids to explore the differences in their relative acidity

- make conclusions about different acids based on observations and measurements made in a number of separate experiments.

YOU WILL NEED:

- five test-tubes • test-tube rack
- samples of dilute sulfuric, citric, hydrochloric and ethanoic acid (all at 1.0 mol/dm³)
- methyl orange • magnesium ribbon • calcium carbonate • copper(II) oxide
- spatula • glass rod • blue litmus paper • stopper and delivery tube • limewater
- safety glasses • lab coat • gloves.

Safety

- Report any acid spills to your teacher immediately.

- Limewater, sulfuric acid and hydrochloric acid are moderate hazards.

- Copper(II) oxide is corrosive, a moderate hazard and harmful to the aquatic environment. Waste from experiments using copper(II) oxide must not be poured down the drain.

- Methyl orange indicator is corrosive, flammable, a health and moderate hazard, hazardous to the aquatic environment, and is acutely toxic.
- If you need to use a hot water-bath to warm the mixture at step 3 of the method, you will need to stand up.
- Citric acid and ethanoic acid are irritants.
- Wear eye protection throughout.

Getting started

Examine the stopper and delivery tube. The stopper will need to be quickly and securely placed over the mouth of the test-tube. Practise fitting the stopper securely and placing the end of the delivery tube into an empty test-tube.

Method

1   Using a pipette, measure $3\,cm^3$ of one of the acids to each of four of the test-tubes.

> **TIP**
>
> Label the test-tubes 1–4 to make it easier to identify which reaction is which.

2   Add a piece of magnesium ribbon to the first tube. Record your observations in your results table in the Recording data section.

3   Add half a spatula of copper(II) oxide to the second tube. If nothing happens, you may need to warm the mixture using a hot water-bath. Record your observations.

4   Half fill a clean test-tube with limewater. Place the end of the delivery tube in the limewater so that the end of the tube is submerged (Figure 11.2). Add half a spatula of calcium carbonate to a test-tube containing acid, and then attach the delivery tube and bubble the gas through limewater. Record your observations.

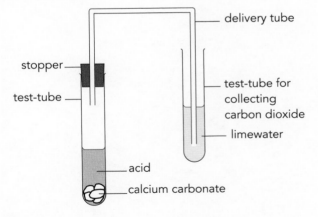

Figure 11.2: Setup for reacting calcium carbonate with acid.

5   Dip the glass rod into tube number 4. Carefully touch the glass rod on to a piece of blue litmus paper. Now add a few drops of methyl orange to the test-tube. Observe and record the colour changes.

6   Pour away the samples in all five tubes and rinse the tubes with water. Repeat steps 1–5 with the other three acids.

Recording data

1   In the space below, draw a table to record your results. You will be collecting the results for four different tests for four types of acid. You will need a heading row and one row for each of the different acids you tested. You will need enough columns to record your results for each test.

Analysis

2   Complete the table.

Test	General result	General word equation
Magnesium		acid + metal → .... + ...
Copper(II) oxide		acid + base → .... + ...
Calcium carbonate		acid + carbonate → .... + ... + ...
Blue litmus		
Methyl orange		

> **TIP**
>
> Bases are oxides or hydroxides of metals. Alkalis are soluble bases.

3   Based on your results, write down the acids in order of the strongest acid to the weakest acid.

....

Evaluation

4   How do you think your results would be different if you had used copper instead of magnesium?

....

....

5   What else could you have used to compare the strength of the acids?

....

Practical investigation 11.3: Investigating relative alkalinity

IN THIS INVESTIGATION YOU WILL:

⟩ identify which of two alkalis is the strongest

- perform a simple titration
- use chemical tests to determine the products produced when reacting alkalis.

YOU WILL NEED:

- dilute sodium hydroxide solution (0.1 mol/dm³)
- calcium hydroxide solution (0.1 mol/dm³) • six test-tubes • universal indicator
- universal indicator chart • red litmus paper • ammonium nitrate solution (0.1 mol/dm³)
- dilute hydrochloric acid (0.1 mol/dm³) • methyl orange • four pipettes
- test-tube rack • forceps • glass rod • beaker (100 cm³ or 250 cm³)
- distilled water • safety glasses • lab coat • gloves.

Safety

- Report any alkali spills to your teacher immediately.
- Dilute sodium hydroxide and calcium hydroxide solution are irritants.
- Hydrochloric acid is a moderate hazard.
- Methyl orange indicator is corrosive, flammable, a health and moderate hazard, hazardous to the aquatic environment, and is acutely toxic.
- Wear eye protection throughout.

Getting started

In this investigation you will be using methyl orange indicator. Methyl orange changes colour in acidic or alkali conditions. Compare this with universal indicator and think about why methyl orange is still useful.

Method

1   Using a pipette, add 2 cm³ of sodium hydroxide solution to three test-tubes and then place these in the test-tube rack. Label the tubes with the name of each test or number them so that you do not get them mixed up.

2   Add a few drops of universal indicator to a test-tube containing sodium hydroxide. Record the colour in the results table in the Recording data section. Pour hydrochloric acid into a beaker until you have approximately 0.5 cm depth. Using a clean pipette, add the hydrochloric acid drop by drop into the test-tube. Stop when the solution has been neutralised. Record the number of drops needed in the results table.

> **TIP**
>
> It is very important to add the hydrochloric acid slowly. Squeeze the pipette until a small droplet of acid appears at the tip and then shake the pipette slightly. Take care that the droplet falls into the bottom of the test-tube and not along the sides of the test-tube.

3 Using a pipette, add $2\,cm^3$ of ammonium nitrate to the next test-tube. Make the red litmus paper damp using distilled water and then hold the paper over the mouth of the test-tube using the forceps. Record the colour change in the results table.

4 Add three drops of methyl orange to the third tube of sodium hydroxide. Record the colour change in the results table.

5 Repeat steps 1–4 using calcium hydroxide.

Recording data

1 Complete the table with your results.

Test	Sodium hydroxide	Calcium hydroxide
Universal indicator colour		
Hydrochloric acid		
Ammonium nitrate / red litmus paper		
Methyl orange		

Analysis

2 Complete the following paragraphs using the words below.

alkalis   ammonium   blue   gas   green

neutralised   purple   yellow

Both of the hydroxides caused universal indicator to change to a .... colour.

This showed us that they are .... When hydrochloric acid was added, the colour

changed to........................... This shows that the alkalis are .... by acids.

When the .... nitrate was added to the alkalis, a reaction took place which

caused ammonia .... to be released. Ammonia is alkaline and this is why the

damp red litmus paper turned .... When methyl orange was added to the

alkalis, the solution turned ....

3 Which of the two alkalis was stronger? What evidence do you have to support your answer?

....

....

Evaluation

4 Which of the tests helped you decide which of the two alkalis was stronger?

....

5 Suggest how you could use universal indicator paper to obtain a pH value for each solution.

....

....

REFLECTION

Think about the different skills you used in this investigation.

How confident are you at measuring volumes accurately, making careful observations and drawing conclusions based on data?

How could you improve your skills?

Practical investigation 11.4: The pH of oxides

IN THIS INVESTIGATION YOU WILL:

- plan an investigation into the differences between basic and acidic oxides by reacting the oxides with acids

- make conclusions on the nature of oxides based on your observations of colour changes.

YOU WILL NEED:

- universal indicator solution • universal indicator colour chart • pipettes
- six test-tubes • test-tube rack • samples of the following solutions: carbon dioxide, sodium oxide, sulfur oxide, phosphorus oxide, potassium oxide, calcium oxide
- safety glasses • lab coat • gloves.

Safety

- Sodium oxide (sodium hydroxide), potassium oxide (potassium hydroxide) and calcium oxide (calcium hydroxide) are all irritants.

- Wear eye protection throughout.

Getting started

You will be using many different samples for the investigation. Before you begin the investigation you should familiarise yourself with the different containers and labels so that you are sure where each substance is.

Think about what you have already learnt about the planning and design of an investigation. Ensure you are familiar with the features that make a good practical method.

Method

1   You need to determine the pH of six different samples using the equipment list given. Plan an investigation and label the diagram to show what you will add to each test-tube (Figure 11.3).

....

....

....

....

....

....

....

....

....

> **TIP**
>
> A white background will help make the colour changes easier to see.

Figure 11.3: Test-tubes for the six different samples.

2   Check your method with your teacher before performing the experiment.

Recording data

3   Record your data in the table below.

Name of oxide	Metal/non-metal	Colour	pH

Analysis

4   Which oxides were acidic?

....

....

5   Which oxides were basic?

....

....

6   Was there a pattern between the type of oxide formed and the pH?

....

....

Evaluation

7   Apart from universal indicator, how else could you have measured the pH of each sample?

....

....

8   Why would it not be suitable to use ether methyl orange or thymolphthalein to measure pH in this investigation?

....

....

EXAM-STYLE QUESTIONS

1 An investigation into the neutralisation of potassium hydroxide by an unknown acid was conducted by two students. The students were trying to determine the temperature change that occurred during the reaction.

They set up an insulated cup and thermometer to measure the temperature change. They measured $25\,cm^3$ of potassium hydroxide and added it to the cup. They then added $5\,cm^3$ of the acid at a time and the temperature of the mixture was recorded.

a **Suggest** a suitable piece of apparatus to use to add the acid.

.... [1]

b Complete the table by reading the temperature from the thermometer diagrams.

COMMAND WORD

suggest: apply knowledge and understanding to situations where there are a range of valid responses in order to make proposals/ put forward considerations

Volume of acid added / cm³	Thermometer diagram	Temperature / °C
0		
5		
10		
15		
20		

CONTINUED

Volume of acid added / cm³	Thermometer diagram	Temperature / °C
25		
30		
35		
40		
45		
50		

[3]

CONTINUED

c   Plot the results of the investigation on the grid below. Add a best-fit line.

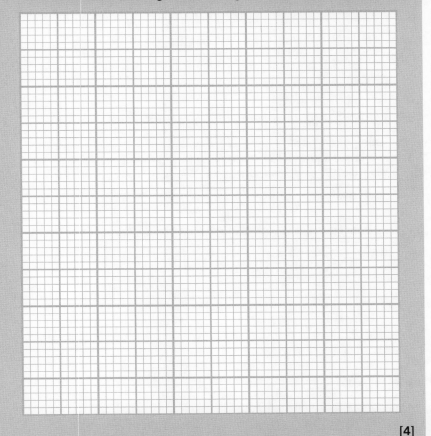

[4]

d   **Analyse** your graph to determine the temperature if 13 cm³ of acid were added.

.... [2]

e   **Examine** the graph to find what volume of acid produced the largest increase in temperature.

.... [2]

[Total: 12]

2   Indicators are important because they can be used to determine whether a substance is an acid or a base. Red cabbage can be used to make an indicator. Suggest a method for preparing a solution from red cabbage that could be used as an indicator. Include details of how you would check to make sure that the indicator works properly.

COMMAND WORDS

analyse: examine in detail to show meaning, identify elements and the relationship between them

examine: investigate closely, in detail

....

....

....

....

.... [5]

3   Design an experiment using the equipment listed below that you could perform to determine which of two alkalis (ammonia solution and potassium hydroxide) is the strongest at the same concentration. You may include a diagram.

Equipment:

- bromothymol blue (this is an indicator that is blue in alkalis but green when neutralised)

- burette and clamp stand

- funnel

- beakers

- conical flask

- measuring cylinders

- alkalis (ammonia solution and potassium hydroxide)

- hydrochloric acid

- white tile.

....

....

....

....

....

....

.... [5]

> Chapter 12

Preparation of salts

THE INVESTIGATIONS IN THIS CHAPTER WILL:

- examine how salts are formed when the hydrogen in an acid is replaced by a metal to form an ionic compound

- show that there are many different types of salts and they are an important part of our day-to-day lives (e.g. fertilisers and food preservatives)

- explore the preparation of soluble salts

- investigate the general solubility rules for salts and enable you to suggest different methods for producing salts

> explore the preparation of insoluble salts.

Practical investigation 12.1: The preparation of soluble salts

KEY WORDS

soluble: a solute that dissolves in a particular solvent

titration: a method of quantitative analysis using solutions; one solution is slowly added to a known volume of another solution using a burette until an endpoint is reached

IN THIS INVESTIGATION YOU WILL:

- prepare soluble salts by the reaction of an acid with a metal, base or carbonate (Method 1) by carefully following a detailed method

- prepare salts by titration of an acid and an alkali (Method 2) by making accurate measurements using a burette.

Method 1: Acid and solid metal, base or carbonate

This method is used when making a salt from a solid metal, a base or a carbonate. An excess of the solid is added to the acid until no more solid will dissolve. Any excess material is filtered out and then the solution is crystallised.

Method 2: Acid and alkali

This method is used when preparing a salt from an acid and an alkali. The acid is titrated into the alkali until neutralisation occurs. The solution is then crystallised. As acids and alkalis can be colourless, it is difficult to see when neutralisation has occurred, so an indicator needs to be used.

YOU WILL NEED:

Method 1
- beaker (250 cm³) • glass rod • funnel • filter paper • Bunsen burner • tripod
- heat-resistant mat • gauze • evaporating basin • measuring cylinder (50 cm³)
- spatula • clamp stand and clamp • tongs • dilute hydrochloric acid (1.0 mol/dm³)
- calcium carbonate • safety glasses • lab coat • gloves.

Method 2
- burette (50 cm³) • measuring cylinder (25 cm³) • clamp stand and clamp • white tile
- funnel • conical flask (100 cm³) • Bunsen burner • tripod • heat-resistant mat • gauze
- evaporating basin • methyl orange indicator • sodium hydroxide solution (1.0 mol/dm³)
- dilute hydrochloric acid (1.0 mol/dm³) • safety glasses • lab coat • gloves.

Safety

- Wear eye protection throughout.

- Sodium hydroxide is corrosive and harmful.

- Hydrochloric acid is a moderate hazard.

- Methyl orange indicator is corrosive, flammable, a health and moderate hazard, hazardous to the aquatic environment, and is acutely toxic.

- Take care when moving hot glassware and use tongs where appropriate.

- Remember to remove the heat from the evaporating basin and do not allow it to boil dry.

- As you will be heating liquids, you will need to stand.

Getting started

Method 2 involves the use of a burette in a titration. A burette is used to accurately dispense a liquid. Make sure you are familiar with the concept of a titration and know to read a burette correctly. See the Practical skills and support section at the start of this workbook for guidance on how to take an accurate measurement of the volume of a liquid.

TIP

Remember that a burette is numbered from top to bottom, so you must read it in the opposite direction from a measuring cylinder.

Method

Method 1

1   Measure 25 cm³ of hydrochloric acid using the measuring cylinder and pour it into the beaker.

2   Add two spatulas of calcium carbonate to the beaker and stir the mixture.

3   Continue adding calcium carbonate until no more of the solid dissolves in the acid.

4   Place the filter paper in the funnel and clamp the funnel above the evaporating basin.

> **TIP**
>
> You can create a cone of filter paper by folding the filter paper in half, then in half again.

5   Carefully pour the solution into the funnel and collect the filtrate in the evaporating basin.

6   Set up the Bunsen burner and tripod. Place the evaporating basin on the gauze and gently heat until the liquid begins to boil. Stop heating when you see crystals begin to form.

7   Use tongs to remove the evaporating basin from the gauze and place the basin on the heat-resistant mat. Allow the evaporating basin to cool.

8   Put the crystals back into a funnel in a filter paper. Wash the crystals carefully with a small amount of distilled water and then put the crystals between two pieces of filter paper so that they can dry.

Method 2

1   Measure 25 cm³ of sodium hydroxide solution using the measuring cylinder and pour the solution into the conical flask.

2   Add five drops of methyl orange indicator to the conical flask.

3   Rinse the burette with distilled water and then rinse the burette with hydrochloric acid. Make sure that the burette is also filled below the tap. Close the burette tap and fill it with hydrochloric acid to a whole number near zero. (It can be zero but does not need to be; just make sure you record the exact value.)

> **TIP**
>
> You may need to shake the burette gently while the tap is open to remove any air bubbles.

4   Secure the burette in the clamp stand. Place the conical flask on a white tile.

5   Slowly add the acid to the alkali in the conical flask a few drops at a time until there is a permanent colour change. You will need to swirl the liquid inside the conical flask after you add each drop of acid.

6   Record the final volume in the burette and calculate the volume you added to neutralise the solution. You now have a known volume of acid needed to neutralise the alkali.

7   Pour away the contents of the conical flask and rinse the flask with water. Add 25 cm³ of sodium hydroxide to the conical flask. Do not add indicator.

8 Refill the burette and then carefully add the known volume of acid from step 6 to the alkali.

9 Once you have added the know volume of acid, remove the conical flask and then add $10\,cm^3$ of the solution to the evaporating basin.

10 Set up the Bunsen burner, tripod and heat-resistant mat. Place the evaporating basin on the gauze and heat the basin until the liquid begins to boil. Once you see crystals forming, turn off the Bunsen burner and allow the basin to cool.

Analysis

1 Write a word equation for the reaction taking place during the preparation of the salt by Method 1.

....

2 Write the balanced symbol equation for this reaction.

....

3 Write a word equation for the reaction taking place during the preparation of the salt by Method 2.

....

4 Write the balanced symbol equation for this reaction.

....

5 Describe the colour change you saw in the conical flask during the titration when the indicator was present.

....

Evaluation

6 Why was the indicator not added to the conical flask when preparing the salts during the second titration?

....

....

7 Why was the solution, formed by reacting calcium carbonate with hydrochloric acid, filtered before it was evaporated?

....

....

8 Describe how you could improve the method for the titration to make sure the volume of acid needed is accurate.

....

....

Practical investigation 12.2: The preparation of insoluble salts

KEY WORDS

insoluble: a substance that does not dissolve in a particular solvent

precipitation: the sudden formation of a solid when either two solutions are mixed or a gas is bubbled into a solution

salts: ionic compounds made by the neutralisation of an acid with a base (or alkali), e.g. copper(II) sulfate and potassium nitrate

IN THIS INVESTIGATION YOU WILL:

> prepare an insoluble salt by precipitation

> record observations about the formation of precipitates.

YOU WILL NEED:

- four test-tubes • test-tube rack • glass rod • distilled water • five pipettes
- sodium carbonate solution (1.0 mol/dm^3) • silver nitrate solution (0.1 mol/dm^3)
- copper(II) sulfate solution (1.0 mol/dm^3) • potassium iodide solution (1.0 mol/dm^3)
- safety glasses • lab coat • gloves.

Safety

- Wear eye protection throughout.
- Copper(II) sulfate is a moderate hazard and harmful to the aquatic environment. Waste from experiments using copper(II) sulfate must not be poured down the drain.
- Silver nitrate solution is a moderate hazard and harmful to the aquatic environment. Waste from experiments using silver nitrate must not be poured down the drain.
- Sodium carbonate is an irritant.
- Potassium iodide is harmful and toxic to the aquatic environment. Waste from experiments using potassium iodide must not be poured down the drain.

Getting started

Look at the names of the compounds you will be using in this investigation. List which elements each compound contains.

Sodium carbonate   ....   Copper(II) sulfate   ....

Silver nitrate   ....   Potassium iodide   ....

Method

1   Rinse each test-tube with distilled water and then place all of the tubes in the test-tube rack.

2   Add about 3 cm³ of sodium carbonate solution to each of the four test-tubes.

3   Add about 3 cm³ of silver nitrate solution to the first tube. Stir using the glass rod.
    Record your observations in the results table in the Recording data section.

4   Add about 3 cm³ of each of the other solutions to the remaining tubes containing sodium
    carbonate and record your observations in the results table.

> **TIP**
>
> Remember to rinse the glass rod each time and use a fresh pipette.

5   Pour away the contents of the test-tubes and rinse them out with distilled water. You will be
    reusing the tubes for the next set of tests so it is very important that the tubes are clean.

6   Repeat steps 2–5 with each of the other solutions so that every combination is completed on the
    results table.

Recording data

1   Fill in the results table with your observations (e.g. 'white precipitate formed' or 'no reaction').

	Silver nitrate	Copper(II) sulfate	Potassium iodide
Sodium carbonate (Tube 1)			
Silver nitrate			
Copper(II) sulfate			

Analysis

2   For each reaction that produced a precipitate, write the word equation and underline the
    precipitate that was visible.

    ....

    ....

    ....

    ....

    ....

....

....

....

3   List the combinations where no precipitate was formed and suggest a reason why.

....

....

Evaluation

4   Why was distilled water used instead of ordinary tap water?

....

5   Suggest a reason for using dilute silver nitrate solution in this investigation.

....

....

REFLECTION

The completed results table will help you learn the general solubility rules for salts. Do you find it easy or difficult to interpret data presented in tables like this?

Are you able to use patterns and relationships to make predictions?

EXAM-STYLE QUESTIONS

1   Two students are trying to make some zinc sulfate crystals. They begin with zinc oxide. They are given the following method by their teacher:

1.   Measure 30 cm³ of dilute sulfuric acid. Add the sulfuric acid to a beaker.

2.   Add one spatula of zinc oxide to the beaker. Stir the beaker and warm the mixture using a hot plate.

3.   Add zinc oxide one spatula at a time to the mixture in the beaker until all of the dilute sulfuric acid has reacted.

4.   Remove any excess zinc oxide.

5.   Collect the crystals of zinc sulfate from the solution.

CONTINUED

COMMAND WORDS

state: express in clear terms

suggest: apply knowledge and understanding to situations where there are a range of valid responses in order to make proposals/ put forward considerations

describe: state the points of a topic / give characteristics and main features

a **State** the apparatus used in step 1 to:

  i Measure the volume of dilute sulfuric acid.

  .... [1]

  ii Stir the mixture.

  .... [1]

b The students were confused by step 3. They were not sure how they would know when all of the dilute sulfuric acid had reacted. **Suggest** how the students would know that all of the sulfuric acid had reacted.

.... [1]

c How is zinc oxide removed in step 4?

.... [1]

d **Describe** the process for collecting crystals in step 5.

....

....

....

....

....

.... [3]

[Total: 7]

2 A student was trying to obtain zinc chloride crystals. They had zinc oxide and hydrochloric acid along with standard laboratory equipment. Describe a method they could use.

....

....

....

....

....

....

.... [5]

> Chapter 13
The Periodic Table

THE INVESTIGATIONS IN THIS CHAPTER WILL:

- look at the changes in reactivity going up or down the groups in the Periodic Table

- use displacement reactions to determine the order of reactivity within a group

> explore trends in properties in groups.

Practical investigation 13.1:
The properties of Group I alkali metals

KEY WORDS

groups: vertical columns of the Periodic Table containing elements with similar chemical properties; atoms of elements in the same group have the same number of electrons in their outer energy levels

period: a horizontal row of the Periodic Table

Periodic Table: a table of elements arranged in order of increasing proton number (atomic number) to show the similarities of the chemical elements with related electronic configurations

IN THIS INVESTIGATION YOU WILL:

- make careful observations of the reactions of the alkali metals and water

- record observations about the effect of the alkali metals on the pH of the water

- predict the reactions of Group I elements from given data.

Safety

- This investigation will be a class demonstration by your teacher. The alkali metals are all very reactive and are therefore too dangerous to be handled by students.

- You will need to wear eye protection throughout the demonstrations and remain behind safety screens.

Getting started

Look at a copy of the Periodic Table. Make sure you are familiar with the arrangement of elements in periods and group. What have you already learnt about the relationship between the properties of different elements and their position in the Periodic Table?

....

....

> **TIP**
>
> The metals in Group I are often called the alkali metals. They are soft solids with relatively low melting points and low densities.

Method

1   Your teacher will first add universal indicator to the water in the trough. The colour should turn green as the water in the trough is neutral.

2   The first metal added to the water will be lithium. Make careful observations of how the lithium reacts once it touches the water. Record any colour change in the water in the results table in the Recording data section.

3   Your teacher will now repeat step 1 with sodium, followed by potassium.

Recording data

1   Record your observations in the results table.

Alkali metal	Observations when added to water	Colour change observed in water
Lithium		
Sodium		
Potassium		

Analysis

2   You will have observed a gas being given off when the alkali metals came into contact with the water. Name the gas produced.

....

3   Write a word equation for the reaction taking place between potassium and water.

.... + ... → .... + ...

4   Based on your results, what effect do the Group I metals have on the pH of the water that they are added to?

....

Evaluation

5   Suggest why rubidium was not used as part of this investigation.

....

6   The colour changes produced by universal indicator are often difficult to observe. Suggest an improvement to the investigation that would enable more accurate data to be collected about pH changes.

....

....

REFLECTION

Some practicals in your chemistry course will be demonstrated by your teacher.
Think about the reasons why a practical may be demonstrated. Do you find observing demonstrations useful?

How could your teacher have improved the demonstration?

....

....

....

Practical investigation 13.2: Investigating the properties and trends of the halogens

IN THIS INVESTIGATION YOU WILL:

- collect qualitative data about the reactivity of the halogens
- compare different halogens with each other on the basis of displacement reactions
- identify trends in halogens.

YOU WILL NEED:

- spotting tile (with at least nine wells) • test-tube rack • rubber stoppers • pipettes
- glass rod • white tile • paper towel • universal indicator paper
- solutions: chlorine water (0.1% w/v), aqueous bromine (0.1% w/v), iodine solution (0.1 mol/dm³), potassium chloride (0.1 mol/dm³), potassium iodide (0.1 mol/dm³), potassium bromide (0.1 mol/dm³) • safety glasses
- lab coat • gloves.

Safety

- Wear eye protection throughout.
- Chlorine water can release chlorine gas so keep the rubber stopper in place. Ensure the laboratory is well ventilated.
- Aqueous bromine is corrosive so wear gloves when handling it.

Getting started

In this investigation you will be using a spotting tile. Practise using a pipette to add three drops of water to each well before the practical. Make sure you dry the spotting tile with a paper towel before starting the investigation.

Method

The effect of halogens on universal indicator paper

TIP

Halogens is a name given to the Group VII elements. They are non-metal elements that are highly reactive.

1   Place three strips of universal indicator paper on the white tile about 3 cm apart. Using a pen, label the universal indicator paper for each halogen you will be testing (bromine, chlorine and iodine).

2   Dip the glass rod into the aqueous bromine and then touch it onto the first piece of universal indicator paper. Record your observations in the first results table in the Recording data section.

3   Wipe the glass rod with a piece of paper towel and then repeat the process with chlorine water on the second strip of universal indicator paper. Record your observations.

4   Wipe the glass rod with paper towel and then repeated the process with iodine solution on the third piece of universal indicator paper. Record your observations. (It may take a few minutes for an effect to be observed. Make sure you wait a few minutes to record any changes.)

Displacement reactions of halogens

1   Using a pencil, label the first column of the spotting tile 'chlorine water'. Label the second column 'aqueous bromine' and the third column 'iodine solution'.

> **TIP**
>
> Use the results table in the Recording data section to help you if you are not sure how to arrange the columns of the spotting tile.

2   Use a pipette to add three drops of chlorine water into each of the wells in the first column.

3   Repeat step 2 for aqueous bromine in column 2 and iodine solution in column 3. Use a clean pipette each time.

4   Use a clean pipette to add three drops of potassium chloride to each of the wells in the first row of the spotting tile. Record any colour changes in the second results table in the Recording data section.

5   Repeat step 4 for row 2 with potassium bromide and row three with potassium iodide. Remember to use a clean pipette for each solution. Record any colour changes.

Recording data

The effect of halogens on universal indicator paper

1   Write your observations of the effect of halogens on universal indicator paper in the results table.

Solution	Observation
Aqueous bromine	
Chlorine water	
Iodine solution	

Displacement reactions of halogens

2   Record your observations of colour changes in the results table.

Solution	Chlorine water	Aqueous bromine	Iodine solution
Potassium chloride			
Potassium bromide			
Potassium iodide			

Analysis

3   Based on your data suggest the order of reactivity for the halogens based on the effect on universal indicator paper.

Most reactive   ....

....

Least reactive   ....

4   Based on the data from the displacement reactions place the halogens in order of most reactive to least reactive.

Most reactive   ....

....

Least reactive   ....

Evaluation

5   Based on the pattern of reactivity you have observed, predict the effect fluorine water would have on universal indicator paper.

....

....

6 Suggest what would happen if potassium fluoride was added to aqueous bromine.

....

....

EXAM-STYLE QUESTIONS

1 Two students are planning to observe the reactions between alkali metals and water demonstrated by their teacher.

a **Suggest** two safety precautions the students should take.

.... [2]

b Metal A was added to the water. A gas was given off during the reaction.

i **State** the name of the gas produced in this reaction.

.... [1]

ii Suggest a test for the gas identified in part **i**. What would be the result of the test?

Test: .... [1]

Result: .... [1]

c The students observed three metals reacting with water and recorded their results shown in the table.

Metal	Observation
A	Violent reaction with water. The metal floats and moves around very quickly on the surface, and a small flame was observed. Gas was produced rapidly and a lilac flame observed.
B	There was a steady reaction with water. A steady stream of gas was given off.
C	There was a fast reaction with water. The metal slowly moved around on the surface of the water. Gas was given off rapidly.

Based on the data, place the metals in order of reactivity from most reactive to least reactive.

Most reactive: ....

....

Least reactive: ....   [2]

COMMAND WORDS

suggest: apply knowledge and understanding to situations where there are a range of valid responses in order to make proposals / put forward considerations

state: express in clear terms

CONTINUED

    d Suggest which of the metals was lithium.

.... [1]

    e Suggest which of the metals was potassium.

.... [1]

[Total: 9]

2 **a** **Describe** an experiment to show that chlorine is more reactive than bromine.

....

....

.... [3]

    b Write the word equation for the reaction you have described in part **a**.

.... [1]

    c State one safety precaution you would take during this experiment.

.... [1]

[Total: 5 marks]

COMMAND WORDS

describe: state the points of a topic / give characteristics and main features

Chapter 14

Metallic elements and alloys

THE INVESTIGATIONS IN THIS CHAPTER WILL:

- explore the general physical properties of metals and non-metals

- examine the chemical properties of metals and their reactions with acids, water and oxygen

- show that metals have different properties that make them well suited to a number of uses, both industrial and domestic.

Practical investigation 14.1: Comparing the general physical properties of metals and non-metals

KEY WORDS

alloy: mixtures of elements (usually metals) designed to have the properties useful for a particular purpose, e.g. solder (an alloy of tin and lead) has a low melting point

electrical conductor: a substance that conducts electricity but is not chemically changed in the process

malleable: a word used to describe the property that metals can be bent and beaten into sheets

metals: a class of chemical elements (and alloys) that have a characteristic shiny appearance and are good conductors of heat and electricity

thermal conductor: a substance that efficiently transfers heat energy by conduction

IN THIS INVESTIGATION YOU WILL:

- explore the physical properties of metals and non-metals by making careful observations

- learn how to identify the type of bonding present in compounds by applying a range of different physical tests

- link the physical properties of metals to their uses.

YOU WILL NEED:

- samples of metal and non-metals • pestle and mortar • light bulb and holder
- battery pack/power pack • three wires with crocodile clips • switch
- safety glasses • lab coat • gloves.

Safety

- Wear eye protection throughout.

- Wash your hands after touching all of the samples.

- Take care not to create a short circuit when testing the conductivity of the samples as a short circuit can damage the battery or power source and cause dangerous sparks.

TIP

A short circuit is caused when the positive and negative wires from a battery or power source touch each other.

Getting started

In this investigation you will need to create a circuit to test whether a sample conducts electricity or not. Using the circuit symbols shown below, draw a circuit diagram to show how you will set up your circuit. Your teacher will check your diagram before you start the experiment.

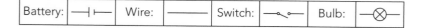

Method

1   Visually inspect one of the sample compounds and record your observations in your results table.

2   You need to set up your simple circuit to test whether the sample conducts electricity. Use your diagram to help you arrange the circuit.

3   Place the sample into your circuit to determine whether the sample conducts electricity. Record your results in your results table. Disconnect the circuit.

4   Touch the sample with your fingers. Does the sample feel cold or warm to the touch? Record your observation in your results table.

5   Place the sample in the mortar and grind the sample with the pestle. Do any parts break off from the sample? Record your results in your results table.

6   Repeat steps 3–5 for each of the different samples you are investigating.

Recording data

1   Create a results table for this experiment.

Think about how many different samples you have to test.

The properties you will be testing are: appearance, conductivity of electricity, conductivity of heat and malleability (whether the substance can change shape without breaking).

Analysis

2   From your results, write the names of the samples in the correct columns in the table below.

Metals	Non-metals

3 Complete the conclusion sentences below for each sample you tested:

a I think that .... is a .... because:

....

....

....

b I think that .... is a .... because:

....

....

....

c I think that .... is a .... because:

....

....

....

d I think that .... is a .... because:

....

....

....

e I think that .... is a .... because:

....

....

....

4 Use the words below to complete the text.

> **brittle   conductors   graphite   grey   heat**
>
> **malleability   metals   non-metals   yellow**

From my investigation I know that the samples that were metals are .... in

colour. The samples that did not have metallic bonding are a variety of colours, including black

and ....

Samples with metallic bonding are good .... of electricity, but

.... work well as insulators. An exception is ...., which is a

good conductor of electricity despite not having metallic bonding.

Samples with metallic bonding are also good conductors of .... as they feel

cold to the touch, while non-metals feel warm to the touch.

.... was tested by hitting the substances with the pestle to see if any parts

broke off. The samples without metallic bonding are .... and so crumble easily.

.... are malleable and can change shape when hit.

Evaluation

5 Why is it difficult to draw conclusions about all substances with metallic and non-metallic bonding based on your investigation?

....

....

....

6 What other tests could you perform on the samples to compare the physical properties of samples with metallic and non-metallic bonding?

....

....

7 The physical properties of different metals make them suitable for particular uses. Which physical properties of copper make it suitable for use in electric wiring? Give one other common use for copper.

Physical properties:

....

Use:

....

8 The physical properties of a metal can be improved by mixing it with other metals. What is a mixture of metals called? Name one example.

A mixture of metals is called:

....

Example:

....

Practical investigation 14.2: The chemical properties of metals

IN THIS INVESTIGATION YOU WILL:

- design a method that is both safe and effective

- make careful observations of the reactions of metals with different acids

- draw conclusions about the chemical properties of metals based on data.

YOU WILL NEED:

- test-tubes • test-tube rack • dilute hydrochloric acid (1.0 mol/dm³)
- dilute sulfuric acid (0.5 mol/dm³) • spatula • pipette • samples of magnesium, zinc, iron, tin and copper • safety glasses • lab coat • gloves.

Safety

- Wear eye protection throughout.

- Sulfuric acid and hydrochloric acid are both moderate hazards.

Getting started

In this investigation you will be using dilute hydrochloric and sulfuric acids. Think about what precautions you will need to take, in order to work safely.

Method

1   For this investigation, you must first plan the method and have it checked by your teacher before starting the experimental work. Your aim is to observe the different metals when they react with the acids, using the equipment list given.

TIP

Number the steps for your method and include as much detail as possible to make the method easy to follow.

....

....

....

....

....
....
....
....
....

Recording data

1   Record your data in the results table.

Metal	Reaction with dilute sulfuric acid	Reaction with dilute hydrochloric acid

Analysis

2   Put the metals in order of increasing reactivity with sulfuric acid from strongest to weakest.

....

....

3   Put the metals in order of increasing reactivity with hydrochloric acid from strongest to weakest.

....

....

4   Name the gas produced in these reactions.

....

5 Suggest which of the two acids is stronger. What evidence do you have to support your answer?

....

....

Evaluation

6 The results you have obtained are descriptive. How could you improve the investigation to obtain numerical data?

....

....

REFLECTION

Evaluate another student's original method for the investigation using the criteria below.

Criteria	Requires improvement	Satisfactory	Excellent
Safety (did they work in a safe way)			
Easy to follow (did they include numbered steps)			
Level of detail (did their method include clear instructions)			
Effectiveness (were they able to obtain sufficient data)			

EXAM-STYLE QUESTIONS

1   One of the ways that materials can be tested to determine if they are metals or non-metals is to see if the material conducts electricity or not. Two students set up a circuit, as in shown in the diagram, and different materials were placed between the crocodile clips. They recorded the current shown on the ammeter. Their data are shown in the table.

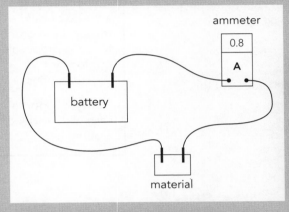

Material	Current / A
A	0.2
B	0.1
C	0.0
D	0.4
E	0.8

a   Construct a graph to show the results.

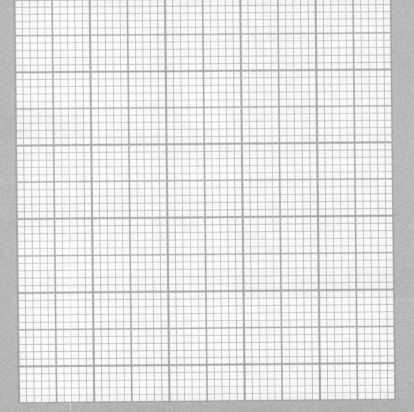

[5]

CONTINUED

COMMAND WORDS

suggest: apply knowledge and understanding to situations where there are a range of valid responses in order to make proposals/ put forward considerations

justify: support a case with evidence/ argument

b One of the materials was a non-metal. Using the information in both the table of results and the graph you have drawn, **suggest** which material it was.

.... [1]

c One of the materials was gold. Using the information in both the table of results and the graph you have drawn, suggest which material it was and **justify** your answer.

.... [1]

d Suggest another circuit component that could have been used in this experiment instead of the ammeter.

.... [1]

e Why is an ammeter a better component to use than your suggestion in **d**?

.... [1]

[Total: 9]

2 Two students were investigating three unknown metals: X, Y and Z. The students plan to perform a number of experiments on the metals.

The first experiment is to place the metals in dilute sulfuric acid. The students placed a piece of each metal into a test-tube. They then added $3\,cm^3$ of dilute sulfuric acid to each tube.

a i Suggest one safety precaution the students must incorporate in their method.

.... [1]

ii **Give** a piece of apparatus the students could use to accurately measure the volume of acid.

.... [1]

COMMAND WORD

give: produce an answer from a given source or recall/ memory

b The students made careful observations of the reactions between the unknown metals and the dilute sulfuric acid. Their observations are recorded in the table.

Metal	Effervescence
X	Vigorous
Y	No reaction
Z	Some bubbles on the surface of the metal

i List the metals in order of most reactive to least reactive.

.... [2]

CONTINUED

ii Suggest a way that the students could have measured the volume of gas produced by each metal.

....

....

.... [1]

iii Name the gas produced when a metal reacts with an acid.

....

....

.... [1]

[Total: 6]

Chapter 15

Reactivity of metals

THE INVESTIGATIONS IN THIS CHAPTER WILL:

- use an electrical current to evaluate the reactivity of metals when they are placed into a circuit with an electrolyte

- use experimental results to deduce the order of reactivity of a set of metals.

Practical investigation 15.1: Investigating the reactivity series of metals

KEY WORDS

electrolyte: an ionic compound that will conduct electricity when it is molten or dissolved in water; electrolytes will not conduct electricity when solid

reactivity series of metals: an order of reactivity, giving the most reactive metal first, based on results from a range of experiments involving metals reacting with oxygen, water, dilute hydrochloric acid and metal salt solutions

IN THIS INVESTIGATION YOU WILL:

deduce an order of reactivity of metals from a given set of experimental results.

YOU WILL NEED:

- sodium chloride solution (2.0 mol/dm³) • strips of four unknown metals A, B, C and D
- two wires with crocodile clips • copper strip • voltmeter • beaker (50 cm³)
- safety glasses • lab coat • gloves.

Safety

Wear eye protection throughout.

Getting started

Look at the voltmeter. Are you able to accurately take readings from the voltmeter? If you have a voltmeter that is not digital then make sure you can work out the value of each of the graduations on the scale.

Method

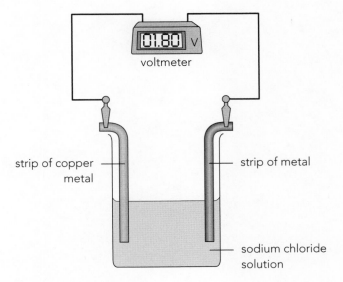

voltmeter

strip of copper metal

strip of metal

sodium chloride solution

Figure 15.1: Setup for testing reactivity of metals.

1 Connect the voltmeter to the two wires as shown in Figure 15.1.

2 Half fill the beaker with sodium chloride solution.

3 Attach the copper strip to one of the crocodile clips. Fold the strip over the edge of the beaker so that it does not move and part of the strip is submerged in the sodium chloride solution.

4 Take unknown metal A and attach it to the other crocodile clip. Fold the strip over the edge of the beaker so that it does not move and part of the strip is submerged in the sodium chloride solution.

5 Record the voltage shown on the voltmeter in your results table.

6 Repeat steps 4 and 5 with each of the unknown metals.

TIP
It is important that the metal strips are clean and free from any dirt or grease so that a good electrical connection can be made.

Recording data

1   Draw a table to record your results.

Handling data

2   Draw a bar graph to show your results.

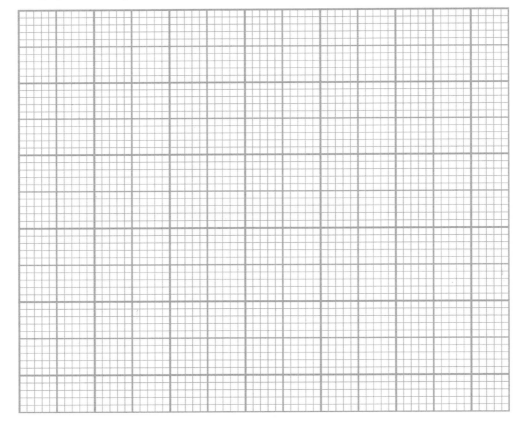

Analysis

3   The more reactive a metal is, the larger the voltage recorded will be. Based on your results, put the unknown metals in order of reactivity from most reactive to least reactive.

....

....

4   The four metals you were given were copper, aluminium, tin and zinc. Using your data and your knowledge of the reactivity series, suggest which the samples were.

A   ....

C   ....

B   ....

D   ....

Evaluation

5   How could you check that the results you obtained for each metal are accurate?

....

....

6   From your results, can you predict the voltage that you would get if you used a strip of magnesium?

....

Practical investigation 15.2: Displacement of metals from salts

KEY WORDS

displacement reaction: a reaction in which a more reactive element displaces a less reactive element from a solution of its salt

IN THIS INVESTIGATION YOU WILL:

- determine a reactivity series of a group of metals by making careful observations of the displacement reaction between metals and metal salts
- use colour changes as evidence for chemical reactions taking place.

YOU WILL NEED:

- spotting tile (either 2× 8 wells or 16 wells) • pipette • beaker (100 cm^3)
- permanent marker • abrasive paper, such as emery paper • solutions: copper(II) sulfate, magnesium sulfate, zinc nitrate, iron sulfate (all 0.5 mol/dm^3) • four pieces of: copper foil, magnesium ribbon, zinc foil (approximately 1 cm long pieces)
- approximately two spatulas of iron filings • safety glasses • lab coat • gloves.

Safety

- Wear eye protection throughout.
- Copper(II) sulfate is a moderate hazard and harmful for the aquatic environment. Waste from experiments using copper(II) sulfate must not be poured down the drain.

Getting started

Think about the different practicals you have seen that have shown different reactivities. Discuss with your partner what you think the order of reactivity for the metals will be in this investigation before you have any data.

Method

1 Use the abrasive paper to rub the surface of each of the metals. The metals will react more easily if the metals are clean.

2 Use the permanent marker to label the spotting tile to match the results table below. See Figure 15.2.

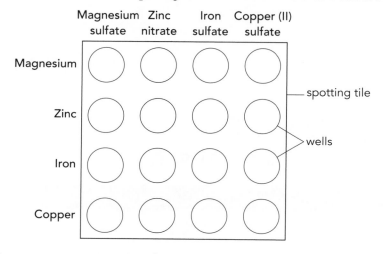

Figure 15.2: How to set out your spotting tile.

3 Place a piece of magnesium in each of the wells in the magnesium row. Repeat with zinc, iron and copper.

4 Using a pipette, add five drops of magnesium sulfate to each of the four wells in the column marked magnesium sulfate.

5 Repeat step 4 with zinc nitrate, iron sulfate and copper(II) sulfate.

6 Observe each well in turn. Use the table in the Recording data section to record which wells show a reaction and which wells do not show a reaction.

> **TIP**
>
> Look for colour changes to show evidence of a reaction.

Recording data

1   Record your data in the table.

	Magnesium sulfate	Zinc nitrate	Iron sulfate	Copper(II) sulfate
Magnesium				
Zinc				
Iron				
Copper				

Analysis

2   Use your results to complete the following sentences:

I think that .... is the most reactive metal because:

....

....

I think that .... is the second most reactive metal because:

....

....

I think that .... is the third most reactive metal because:

....

....

I think that .... is the least reactive metal because:

....

....

> **TIP**
>
> Refer to the actual results from your results table in your answers.

Evaluation

3 Suggest why some of the metals changed colour.

....

....

4 Suggest why some of the metals did not change colour.

....

....

REFLECTION

Think about the following questions:

Were your predictions in the Getting started section correct?

What factors did you consider when making your predictions?

Do you feel confident in predicting the outcome of investigations?

EXAM-STYLE QUESTIONS

1 A student is investigating the reactivity of different metals (as shown in the diagram). He wants to measure how much gas is given off in one minute when he adds each metal to $20\,cm^3$ of sulfuric acid. The gas produced during the reaction will be collected in an inverted measuring cylinder. Each metal is carefully cleaned before the experiment.

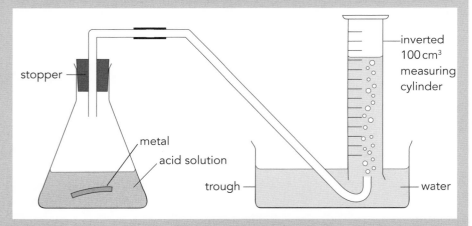

a **Suggest** a piece of apparatus the student could use to time one minute.

.... [1]

COMMAND WORD

suggest: apply knowledge and understanding to situations where there are a range of valid responses in order to make proposals/ put forward considerations

CONTINUED

b Look at the measuring cylinder diagrams below. Draw a table and record the volume of gas produced by each metal in one minute.

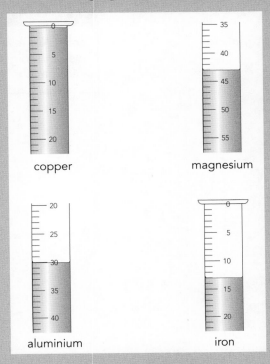

copper   magnesium

aluminium   iron

[6]

CONTINUED

c How could he have obtained more accurate data for the volume of gas produced?

.... [1]

d **Consider** why the metals were cleaned before the experiment.

.... [1]

COMMAND WORD

consider: review and respond to given information

e Using the data, plot a graph to show the results.

[4]

f Using the results table and your graph, put the metals in order of reactivity starting with the most reactive.

....

....

....

.... [3]

The student repeated the experiment with an unidentified metal. It produced the result shown in the diagram.

g   Using the data and your answer to part **f**, suggest which metal this might be. **Justify** your answer.

....

.... [2]

h   What is the name of the gas being produced?

.... [1]

i   How could you test the gas and what result would you expect to see if your suggestion in **h** is correct?

....

.... [2]

j   The student did not control all of the variables in his experiment. **Evaluate** the experiment and name the two variables that he did not control. Suggest how he could improve his method to make sure that these variables are controlled.

....

....

....

....

....

.... [4]

[Total: 25]

COMMAND WORDS

justify: support a case with evidence/ argument

evaluate: judge or calculate the quality, importance, amount, or value of something

CONTINUED

2 The reactivity series can be used to predict if one metal will displace another from a solution of one of its salts. This reaction will release energy in the form of heat.

Two students wanted to investigate the temperature changes that occurred when they added different metals to lead sulfate. They followed the method described below.

Using a pipette, 25 cm³ of lead sulfate was added to a glass beaker. The temperature of the lead sulfate was measured using a glass thermometer. A spatula of magnesium powder was added to the beaker and the mixture was stirred. The highest temperature reached was recorded. This method was repeated with zinc, iron and copper powder.

a Suggest three improvements to the method described above.

....

....

....

.... [3]

b Look at the results table below. Add the name of the metal powder that you think caused each temperature change. The starting temperature of the lead sulfate was 24 °C.

Metal powder	Highest temperature reached / °C
	38
	24
	28
	41

[4]

[Total: 7]

> Chapter 16

Extraction and corrosion of metals

THE INVESTIGATIONS IN THIS CHAPTER WILL:

- show the process and chemistry of extracting iron and copper
- complete small-scale versions of large industrial processes used to extract different metals from their ores
- explore how the reactivity series is used in the extraction of metals from their ores
- look at the causes of rusting and show how different methods can be used to prevent rusting.

Practical investigation 16.1: Producing iron from iron oxide

KEY WORDS

blast furnace: a furnace for extracting metals (particularly iron) by reduction with carbon that uses hot air blasted in at the base of the furnace to raise the temperature

ore: a naturally occurring mineral from which a metal can be extracted

reduction: there are three definitions of reduction:
i   a reaction in which oxygen is removed from a compound
ii a reaction involving the gain of electrons by an atom, molecule or ion
iii a reaction in which the oxidation state of an element is decreased

IN THIS INVESTIGATION YOU WILL:

- follow a method carefully to enable you to produce iron from iron oxide
- use the process of reduction to remove oxygen from iron oxide
- make links between the small-scale reduction of iron oxide and the large-scale industrial process for the extraction of iron from iron ore.

YOU WILL NEED:

- sodium carbonate powder • iron(III) oxide powder • match • tongs
- Bunsen burner • heat-resistant mat • magnet • resealable plastic bag
- pestle and mortar • white paper • safety glasses • lab coat • gloves.

Safety

- Wear eye protection throughout.
- Sodium carbonate powder is an irritant.

Getting started

This investigation uses a small-scale practical to make links with the industrial extraction of iron from iron ore (hematite) in the blast furnace. Read the section on the production of iron in the blast furnace in Chapter 16 in the Coursebook to make sure you are familiar with the basic steps in the large-scale process.

Method

1 Moisten the head of the match with water.

2 Roll the head of the match in the sodium carbonate powder.

3 Roll the head of the match in the iron(III) oxide powder.

4 Set up the Bunsen burner on the heat-resistant mat.

5 Light the Bunsen burner and set it to a blue flame.

6 Pick up the match with the tongs and hold it in the flame. Allow the match to burn halfway along the length before blowing it out.

> **TIP**
>
> It can sometimes be difficult to pick up the match using the tongs. Hold the match in one hand and then, using the tongs in your other hand, close the tongs to grip the match.

7 Turn off the Bunsen burner and allow the match to cool on the heat-resistant mat.

8 Place the charred (burnt) part of the match in the mortar and grind it with the pestle for a few seconds until you have a fine powder.

9 Seal the magnet in the plastic bag and then dip the magnet into the powder. Remove the magnet from the powder and then blow gently to remove any loose material.

10 Hold the bag over white paper and remove the magnet. Look for any pieces that have fallen from the bag.

Analysis

1   What were the small black specks that you saw on the white paper when you removed the magnet?

....

....

2   What was the source of carbon in the reaction?

....

....

3   Write the word equation for the reaction taking place.

....

....

Evaluation

4   Why was a match used for this investigation?

....

....

5   What is the name given to this type of reaction?

....

REFLECTION

How did this small-scale practical help your understanding of the role of the following in the blast furnace method for the production of iron: coke, iron ore and hot air blast?

Do you understand how the steps in the experiment relate to the large-scale process?

Do you think small-scale experiments are useful?

....

....

....

....

Practical investigation 16.2: Producing copper from copper(II) carbonate

IN THIS INVESTIGATION YOU WILL:

- use a variety of equipment safely to enable you to separate copper from copper(II) carbonate

- link your practical results to the reactions that take place in the industrial extraction of copper from copper ore

- evaluate the different chemicals and methods you are using.

YOU WILL NEED:

- Bunsen burner • heat-resistant mat • tripod • clay triangle • crucible
- spatula • copper(II) carbonate • powdered carbon • beaker (250 cm³) • tongs
- safety glasses • lab coat • gloves.

Safety

- Wear eye protection throughout.

- Copper(II) carbonate is harmful if swallowed, is an irritant and is harmful to the aquatic environment. Waste from experiments using copper(II) carbonate must not be poured down the drain.

- The crucible will be very hot so you will need to grip the crucible with the tongs carefully and make sure you do not touch it with your hands.

Getting started

The crucible can be very delicate. Practise placing the crucible in the clay triangle on top of a tripod. Ensure that the crucible is secure in the clay triangle and does not move. You will also need to decide how you will place the clay triangle on the tripod so that it is secure.

Method

1   Set up the tripod with the clay triangle on the heat-resistant mat.

2   Add two spatulas of the copper(II) carbonate powder to the crucible. Place the crucible in the clay triangle.

3   Light the Bunsen burner and carefully heat the crucible on a blue flame. Look for a colour change from green to black.

4   Allow the crucible to cool for five minutes.

5   Add three spatulas of carbon powder to the crucible. Use the tongs to hold the edge of the crucible to stop it from moving, and then stir the contents using the spatula. Make sure that the two powders are well mixed.

6   Add one more spatula of carbon powder to the crucible. Carefully sprinkle this over the surface to form a layer on the top of the mixture.

7   Heat the crucible using a blue flame and then change to a roaring flame until the reaction mixture glows orange.

8   Turn off the Bunsen burner and allow the crucible to cool.

9   Half fill the beaker with water.

10 Holding the crucible with the tongs, pour the powder from the crucible into the beaker.

11 Stir the contents of the beaker with the spatula and allow the sediment to settle. The copper is more dense than water and carbon, so it should sink to the bottom of the beaker. Carefully pour off the water, which should contain a black suspension of carbon powder. Add more water and repeat this step until only the heavy material remains at the bottom of the beaker.

> **TIP**
>
> Be careful not to pour the water out of the beaker too quickly as the copper can also be poured away by accident.

Analysis

1   Write the word equation for the reaction that took place when you heated the copper(II) carbonate.

   ....

2   What is the symbol equation for this reaction?

   ....

3   Write the word equation for the reaction that took place when you heated the copper oxide with the carbon.

   ....

4   What is the symbol equation for this reaction?

   ....

Evaluation

5   Why did the copper sink to the bottom of the water?

   ....

   ....

6 What was the purpose of the carbon powder?

....

....

7 Aluminium is a more reactive metal than copper and so cannot be extracted from its ore (bauxite) by reduction with carbon. Suggest a technique that could be used to extract aluminium from bauxite.

....

....

Practical investigation 16.3: What causes rusting?

KEY WORD

rust: a loose, orange–brown, flaky layer of hydrated iron(III) oxide, $Fe_2O_3 \cdot xH_2O$, found on the surface of iron or steel

IN THIS INVESTIGATION YOU WILL:

- compare different environmental conditions and the impact they have on rusting

- plan an experiment to determine the causes of rusting, exploring many different variables.

YOU WILL NEED:

- four test-tubes • four iron nails • distilled water • test-tube rack • boiled water
- oil • anhydrous calcium chloride (approximately 2 g) • stopper • salt solution
- three pipettes • spatula • permanent marker pen • safety glasses • lab coat
- gloves.

Safety

- Wear eye protection throughout.
- The iron nails may be sharp so take care with these.
- Anhydrous calcium chloride is an irritant.

Getting started

You will need to decide what to put in each of your test-tubes to see what causes rusting to occur. When making your decision, you should consider the following points:

- Boiled water will contain very little oxygen.

- A layer of oil prevents oxygen entering water.
- Anhydrous calcium chloride removes water from the air.
- Salt water makes rusting happen faster.

Predict under which conditions rusting will occur fastest.

....

Method

1   Complete the table below to show what you will put in each tube and which of the following three variables each tube will contain.

oxygen   salt   water

Tube number			
1	2	3	4
Contents			
Variable present			

2   Now that you have decided what each tube will contain, write a numbered method for the investigation using the equipment list given.

....

....

....

....

....

....

....

....

....

....

The teacher will check your method before performing the experiment.

TIP

Remember that you will need to number each test-tube.

Recording data

1 Design a table to record your results.

Analysis

2 Which nail rusted the most?

....

....

3 Which nails rusted least?

....

....

4 Explain the reasons for the results you observed. Which variables caused the most and least rusting? Can you explain the reasons for the results you observed using your knowledge of chemistry? Complete the sentences below.

The most rusting was caused by .... because:

....

....

The least rusting was caused by .... because:

....

....

5   Based on the results of your experiment, which factors increase rusting?

....

....

Evaluation

6   What could you have done as a control for this investigation?

....

....

7   Suggest what would happen if you were to repeat this investigation using copper nails.
Explain your answer.

....

....

....

....

REFLECTION

Look at the predictions you made at the start of the investigation. Evaluate how good
your predictions were. Was your reasoning correct?

Do you feel confident making predictions based on your background knowledge
of chemistry?

....

....

Practical investigation 16.4: Preventing rusting

KEY WORDS

corrosion: the process that takes place when metals and alloys are chemically attacked by
oxygen, water or any other substances found in their immediate environment

galvanising: the protection of iron and steel objects by coating with a layer of zinc

sacrificial protection: a method of rust protection involving the attachment of blocks of a
metal more reactive than iron to a structure; this metal is corroded rather than the iron or
steel structure

IN THIS INVESTIGATION YOU WILL:

- use a variety of different techniques to prevent rusting

- make conclusions based on the data you have obtained.

YOU WILL NEED:

- magnesium ribbon • copper foil • eight test-tubes • six iron nails • acrylic paint
- test-tube rack • corrosion indicator • grease/petroleum jelly • plastic wrap/food wrap
- permanent marker pen • galvanised nail • safety glasses • lab coat • gloves.

Safety

Wear eye protection throughout.

Getting started

You will be using magnesium and copper foil in this experiment. What have you already learnt about the reactivity of magnesium and copper?

....

....

Method

1   Place the eight test-tubes in the test-tube rack. Label them 1–8 with the permanent marker.

2   Paint one of the iron nails with the acrylic paint and leave the nail to dry.

3   Leave test-tube 1 empty and place an iron nail in the tube labelled 2.

4   Cover one of the other iron nails in the grease/petroleum jelly. Place this in tube 3.

5   Wrap a piece of magnesium ribbon around an iron nail and place it in tube 4.

6   Wrap a piece of copper foil around an iron nail and then place it in tube 5.

7   Carefully wrap an iron nail in the plastic wrap. Make sure that there are no holes. Place this nail in tube 6.

8   Place the painted iron nail in tube 7.

9   Place the galvanised nail in tube 8.

10   Add the corrosion indicator to each of the tubes so that the nail is completely covered.

11   Leave the tubes for 30 minutes and then record your observations in your results table. (You will need to design your data collection table in the Recording data section.)

Recording data

1 Design a results table to record your observations.

> **TIP**
>
> Make sure you include a column in your table for the colour change of the corrosion indicator.

Handling data

2 Use your results to complete the following table.

Tubes where corrosion occurred	Tubes where no corrosion occurred

Analysis

3 In which tubes was corrosion prevented by stopping oxygen from coming into contact with the iron?

....

....

4 Why was magnesium ribbon better at preventing corrosion than copper foil? Look back at your answers to the Getting started section to help you.

....

....

5 Give an example of how each method of rust prevention is used in real life.

 a Plastic coating

....

 b Painting

....

 c Grease

....

 d Galvanising

....

 e Sacrificial protection

....

See Chapter 16 in the Coursebook for more information on methods of rust prevention.

Evaluation

6 Why was one tube filled with only the corrosion indicator?

....

....

7 If the test-tube with just the corrosion indicator also changed colour, what would this tell us about the reliability of our investigation?

....

....

8 Suggest why there may still be some corrosion even in the tubes with nails that have been treated with grease, paint or plastic.

....

....

9 Electroplating is often used to prevent rusting. Explain how you could use electroplating to protect an iron nail from corrosion.

....

....

....

....

REFLECTION

Question 5 asks you to give examples of methods of rust prevention that are used in real life. Are you able to relate the background chemistry to the real-life examples?

How does referring to real-life examples help your learning?

....

....

EXAM-STYLE QUESTIONS

1   Two students have a sample of copper(II) carbonate. Their teacher has asked them to plan an experiment to produce some pure copper from the copper(II) carbonate. They have the following equipment:

Bunsen burner, boiling tube, carbon powder, spatula, test-tube holder, heat-resistant mat

   a   Write a short plan for how they could obtain pure copper using the apparatus given.

....

....

....

....

.... [4]

   b   Write word equations for the reactions taking place in your method.

....

.... [6]

   c   The copper obtained from using the reduction method is not pure. **Suggest** what further steps the students would have to take to obtain pure copper.

....

....

....

....

.... [3]

COMMAND WORD

suggest: apply knowledge and understanding to situations where there are a range of valid responses in order to make proposals/ put forward considerations

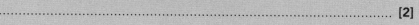

CONTINUED

d Suggest two uses of copper.

.... [2]

[Total: 15]

2 Two students are investigating rusting. They have set up the experiment shown in the diagram to investigate how different variables affect whether an iron nail will rust or not.

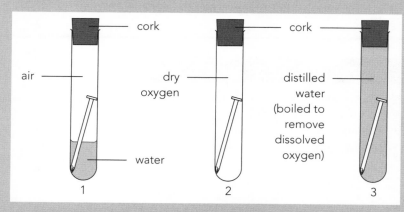

a **Predict** which of the tubes rust will appear in first.

.... [1]

b **Explain** your prediction.

....

.... [2]

c Predict which of the tubes rust will appear in last.

.... [1]

d Explain your prediction.

....

.... [2]

In another investigation, the students are investigating sacrificial protection of iron. They have five metal strips which they will wrap around an iron nail. The nail will then be placed in water that contains oxygen.

> COMMAND WORDS

predict: suggest what may happen based on available information

explain: set out purposes or reasons / make the relationships between things evident / provide why and/or how and support with relevant evidence

CONTINUED

e   In the box below, suggest which of the metals would protect the iron nail from rusting and which would not.

Metals: zinc, copper, tin, magnesium, lead

Metals that would protect an iron nail from rusting	Metals that would not protect an iron nail from rusting

[5]

f   Explain the reasons for your suggestions above.

....

.... [2]

[Total: 13]

3   Car engines become very hot when they are in use, which is why they have a cooling system. Part of the system is a radiator, which transfers heat to the surroundings. The radiator usually contains water. Radiators are normally made of steel and so they are prone to rusting. Coolant additives can be poured into the radiator to reduce rusting

You have been given four different types of coolant additive to test. Small strips of metal for making the steel radiator have also been provided. Plan an investigation to determine which of the coolant additives works best at preventing rusting.

....

....

....

....

....

....

....

....

....

.... [10]

> Chapter 17

Chemistry of the environment

THE INVESTIGATIONS IN THIS CHAPTER WILL:

- enable you to calculate the percentage of oxygen in the air

- explore the impact that acid rain has on a variety of different metals

- use models to simulate the earth's atmosphere to show that carbon dioxide is a contributory factor to climate change

- develop methods for combating the damage caused to the environment by acid rain

- test the purity of water using multiple techniques.

Practical investigation 17.1: Estimating the percentage of oxygen in air

IN THIS INVESTIGATION YOU WILL:

- make careful measurements of the change in volume of gases by measuring the displacement of water

- use data to calculate the percentage of oxygen in air.

YOU WILL NEED:

- iron wool • boiling tube • rubber stopper • beaker (250 cm^3)
- measuring cylinder (25 cm^3) • glass rod • permanent marker pen • safety glasses
- lab coat • gloves.

Safety

- Wear eye protection throughout.

- Take care when handling glassware.

Getting started

As part of this practical you will need to place a boiling tube upside down in a beaker of water. This is a difficult procedure so practise this part of the method (steps 2–5) a few times with just water in the boiling tube. If you have completed the procedure correctly the boiling tube should still be half full of water.

Method

1   Place a piece of iron wool into the bottom of the boiling tube. The piece of iron wool needs to be large enough so that is does not move when the boiling tube is turned upside down.

> **TIP**
>
> You can use the glass rod to help you push the iron wool to the bottom of the boiling tube.

2   Pour water into the boiling tube until it is half full so that the iron wool is completely covered. Place the rubber stopper on the boiling tube.

3   Fill the beaker with approximately $150\,cm^3$ of water.

4   Invert the boiling tube and place it into the beaker. Hold the stopper in place while you do this to avoid the stopper falling out.

5   Carefully remove the stopper from the boiling tube (Figure 17.1).

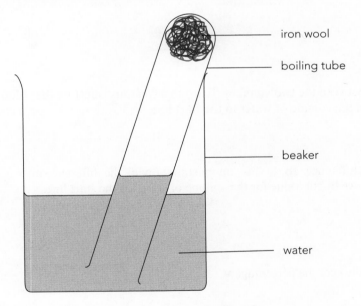

Figure 17.1: Setup to measure oxygen in the air using iron wool.

6   Using the marker pen, draw a line to mark how far the column of air is on the boiling tube. Label this line with the word 'start'.

7   Leave the experiment for one week.

8 Using the marker pen, a draw a line to mark the new position of the column of air. Label this line with the word 'finish'.

9 Carefully remove the boiling tube from the beaker.

10 Fill the boiling tube with water up to the line you labelled 'start'. Now pour the water into a measuring cylinder. Record this value in the table below.

11 Empty the measuring cylinder and then fill the boiling tube with water to the line labelled 'finish'.

12 Pour the water into a measuring cylinder.

Recording data

Because the water will have the same volume as the air inside the tube, by measuring the volume of water you will also be measuring the volume of air that was inside the tube.

1 Use the table to record your data.

Volume to start line / cm³	Volume to finish line / cm³

2 What are your observations of the iron wool inside the tube?

....

....

Handling data

3 Now calculate the difference between the two volumes. To do this you must subtract the volume of water to the finish line from the volume of water to the start line.

difference in volume = ...

4 Now calculate the percentage difference. To do this you must first divide the difference in volume that you calculated above by the value for the volume of water to the start line.

$$\frac{\text{difference in volume}}{\text{volume at start}} = ...$$

5 Now multiply this value by 100 to get the percentage = ...%

Analysis

6 Use the words below to complete the sentences. Use your own results to complete the conclusion.

difference   iron   iron oxide   oxygen   rusting   volume   water

The reaction that took place was called .... This is the name for the oxidation

of ....

Oxygen from the atmosphere reacted with the iron wool to form a new compound called

.... or rust. At the start of the investigation the air in the tube contained

.... but by the end of the investigation this had all gone as it had reacted with

the iron. As the oxygen had been removed from the air the .... of gas inside

the tube was lower. This meant that .... from the beaker moved up inside the

boiling tube.

By measuring the .... in the volume of gas from start to finish, it was possible

to calculate the volume of oxygen that had been removed from the air in the tube. This was then

calculated to be .... %.

Evaluation

7 Apart from the decrease in the volume of gas inside the tube, what other evidence was there for a reaction having taken place?

....

....

8 Why did the experiment have to be left for one week?

....

....

9 What other apparatus could you have used to measure more precisely the volume of oxygen being used up?

....

....

10 The real percentage of oxygen in clean dry air is approximately 21%. Look at your estimate. Suggest why your estimated value was higher or lower than the real value.

....

....

....

....

11 Use the knowledge you have gained from this investigation and your general chemistry knowledge to suggest a method for estimating the percentage of carbon dioxide in the air.

....

....

....

....

....

REFLECTION

Think about the different practical skills and techniques you have learnt. Does practising the techniques help you to improve your skills?

What other methods could you use to improve your skills?

....

....

....

Practical investigation 17.2: The effects of acid rain on metal

KEY WORDS

acid rain: rain that has been made more acidic than normal by the presence of dissolved pollutants such as sulfur dioxide (SO_2) and oxides of nitrogen (nitrogen oxides, NO_x)

IN THIS INVESTIGATION YOU WILL:

* make observations of the effects of acid rain on metals

* develop your ability to gather appropriate data by deciding on the number of repeat readings to collect.

YOU WILL NEED:

* zinc foil • tin foil • iron sheet • magnesium ribbon • copper foil • foam sheet
* plastic box with lid • beaker (100 cm³) • scissors • measuring cylinder (50 cm³)
* marker pen • sandpaper • safety glasses • lab coat • gloves.

Safety

* Wear eye protection throughout.
* Make sure that you do not remove the acid solution or the plastic boxes from the fume cupboard.
* Sulfur dioxide is toxic. Do not remove the sulfur dioxide solution from the fume cupboard.
* Do not open the plastic box once you have placed the beaker of acid inside the box.

Getting started

You will be using a sulfur dioxide solution to create an acidic atmosphere inside a container to determine which metals are most affected by acid rain. Think about the chemistry behind the formation of acid rain and the reactions of acids with metals. Familiarise yourself with each type of metal used in the investigation so that you able to identify it. Based on your knowledge of the reactivity of metals, think about which metals will be affected the most by acid rain and which metals will be affected the least.

Method

1   Place the foam sheet in the plastic box. You might need to use the scissors to cut the sheet to the correct shape. Use the marker pen to label the lid with the name of each metal.

TIP

Make sure the labels are spaced apart so that you have enough space to insert all of the metal samples.

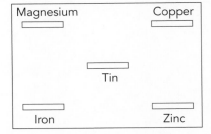

Figure 17.2: A plan of how to set out the metal samples in the foam tray.

2   Carefully clean each piece of metal with the sandpaper and insert each piece into the foam so that the metal is standing upright. Ensure that each metal is next to the label you have written. Make sure each metal strip is secure and will not fall over.

3   Take the plastic box to the fume cupboard with the $100\,cm^3$ beaker.

4   Carefully measure $30\,cm^3$ of sulfur dioxide solution using the measuring cylinder and pour this into the $100\,cm^3$ beaker.

5   Place the beaker with the sulfur dioxide solution into the plastic box and seal the lid tightly.

6   Leave the plastic box inside the fume cupboard and return to the cupboard periodically to observe the effects of the sulfur dioxide on the metals.

Recording data

1   In the space below, design a results table that includes space for the names of each metal and space to record your observations of the effect of the sulfur dioxide solution. Ask your teacher how many times you should observe the results.

Analysis

2 From your observations, which of the metals were most corroded by the acidic environment?

....

....

3 Which of the metals corroded first?

....

4 Why do you think that this metal corroded first?

....

....

5 Were there any metals that did not corrode?

....

6 Why do you think that these metals did not corrode?

....

....

Evaluation

7 Suggest why it was necessary to clean the metals with sandpaper at the start of the investigation.

....

....

8 Why was it possible to see corrosion on many of the metals in this investigation in only a few days when building materials can last for many years in areas where there is acid rain?

....

....

....

9 What is the main source of sulfur dioxide in the environment?

....

....

10 How could you have designed a control for this investigation?

....

....

....

REFLECTION

What have you learnt in this investigation about the importance of making repeat observations?

Making observations is part of the 'scientific method'. What do you understand by the 'scientific method'?

How can the 'scientific method' help you to evaluate an investigation and suggest improvements?

....

....

Practical investigation 17.3: The effect of carbon dioxide on the atmosphere

KEY WORDS

antacids: compounds used medically to treat indigestion by neutralising excess stomach acid

greenhouse effect: the natural phenomenon in which thermal energy from the Sun is 'trapped' at the Earth's surface by certain gases in the atmosphere (greenhouse gases)

greenhouse gas: a gas that absorbs heat reflected from the surface of the Earth, stopping it escaping the atmosphere

IN THIS INVESTIGATION YOU WILL:

- examine how modelling can be used to provide data
- learn about the effects of carbon dioxide on the Earth's atmosphere (greenhouse effect).

YOU WILL NEED:

- two large clear plastic drinks bottles (at least 1.5 dm³) • two thermometers
- two rubber stoppers with holes for thermometers (or modelling clay) • lamp
- metre ruler • measuring cylinder (1000 cm³ or 500 cm³) • two antacid tablets
- marker pen • safety glasses • lab coat • gloves.

Safety

- Wear eye protection throughout.
- The lamp may become hot as it will be on for a long time.
- Take care with thermometers as they can break very easily.

Getting started

This investigation will investigate carbon dioxide as a greenhouse gas. Look at the equipment used to model the greenhouse effect. Read the sections on global warming and the greenhouse effect in Chapter 17 in the Coursebook, and think about which parts of the equipment are used to model the Sun, the atmosphere and fossil fuels.

Method

1   Using the measuring cylinder, measure $750\,cm^3$ of water into each of the bottles. Label one bottle 'Carbon dioxide' and the other bottle 'Normal air'.

2   Insert the thermometers into the stoppers or use the modelling clay to create a lid for each bottle with the thermometer suspended inside.

3   Measure the temperature of the air in both bottles.

4   Add the antacid tablets to the water in the 'Carbon dioxide' bottle and close the bottle immediately with the stopper or modelling clay.

> **TIP**
>
> It is important that both bottles are sealed well so that they are airtight.

5   Place the lamp 40 cm from the bottles and switch it on.

6   After 45 minutes, record the temperature in each bottle again.

Recording data

1   Record your data in the table.

Bottle	Temperature at start / °C	Temperature at end / °C
Carbon dioxide		
Normal air		

Handling data

2 Use the data from your results to plot a bar chart.

> **TIP**
>
> You will need to label your x-axis with a space for start and end temperatures for both carbon dioxide and normal air. This means that you will have four bars in total.

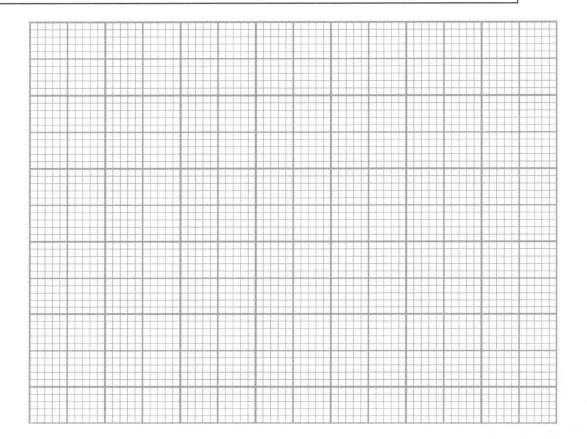

Analysis

3 For each of the two bottles, calculate the temperature change from the start to the end of the experiment.

Bottle	Temperature change from start to end / °C
Carbon dioxide	
Normal air	

4   Look at your results. What can you conclude from your investigation about the effect of carbon dioxide on the temperature of the gas inside the bottle?

....

....

....

Evaluation

5   List at least three variables in this experiment that you controlled.

....

....

6   How could you test the gas produced by antacid tablets to make sure it is carbon dioxide?

....

....

7   Why is it important that both bottles are the same distance from the lamp?

....

....

8   What would be the effect on the temperature of a bottle that was placed closer to the lamp?

....

....

9   How could you redesign this experiment to determine whether increasing carbon dioxide concentration increased the change in temperature?

....

....

....

REFLECTION

The greenhouse effect and the associated changes in climate have wide-ranging social, economic and environmental implications. Do small-scale laboratory experiments help you to understand the background chemistry involved in global warming?

....

....

Practical investigation 17.4: Testing the purity of water

KEY WORDS

lime: a white solid known chemically as calcium oxide (CaO), produced by heating limestone; it can be used to counteract soil acidity, to manufacture calcium hydroxide (slaked lime) and also as a drying agent

limestone: a form of calcium carbonate ($CaCO_3$)

IN THIS INVESTIGATION YOU WILL:

- use a variety of experimental techniques to confirm your conclusions
- determine the purity of water by measuring melting and boiling points.

YOU WILL NEED:

- Bunsen burner • tripod • gauze • heat-resistant mat
- two evaporating basins • thermometer • two beakers ($250\,cm^3$)
- two measuring cylinders ($25\,cm^3$ and $100\,cm^3$) • water samples A and B for testing
- ice cubes • marker pen • safety glasses • lab coat • gloves • balance.

Safety

- Wear eye protection throughout.
- Do not boil the evaporating basins or beakers until they are dry.

Getting started

Think about why water purity is important. With a partner, discuss a situation you could find yourself in where you might need to test the purity of water.

Method

This investigation contains three separate methods. The methods can be attempted in any order.

Testing the melting point of water

1   Add 4–5 cubes of ice into a beaker.

2   Using the $100\,cm^3$ measuring cylinder collect $50\,cm^3$ of water sample A.

3   Carefully pour the water into the beaker with the ice cubes.

4   Take the thermometer and place it into the beaker with the ice. Leave it for one minute. Record the temperature of the melting ice in the results table in the Recording data section.

5   Empty the beaker and rinse it thoroughly.

6   Repeat steps 1–4 with water sample B.

Testing the boiling point of water

1   Using the $100\,cm^3$ measuring cylinder collect $50\,cm^3$ of water sample A.

2   Pour the sample into a beaker.

3   Set up a tripod and gauze on a heat-resistant mat. Connect a Bunsen burner to the gas supply and light the Bunsen burner.

4   Place the beaker containing water sample A onto the gauze.

5   Heat the beaker on a cool blue flame until the water begins to boil.

6   Using the thermometer, measure the temperature of the boiling water.

7   Record your result in the results table in the Recording data section.

8   Once the beaker has cooled, empty the beaker and rinse it thoroughly.

9   Repeat steps 1–8 with water sample B.

Testing for dissolved substances

1   Use the marker pen to label the evaporating basins A and B. Use the weighing scale to measure the mass of each evaporating basin. Record the mass of the evaporating basins in the results table in the Recording data section.

2   Using a measuring cylinder collect $25\,cm^3$ of water sample A.

3   Set up a tripod and gauze on a heat-resistant mat. Connect a Bunsen burner to the gas supply.

4   Pour the water from the measuring cylinder into the evaporating basin. Place the evaporating basin onto the gauze.

5   Light the Bunsen burner and heat the evaporating basin on a cool blue flame until nearly all of the water has evaporated. Do not heat the evaporating basin until it is completely dry.

6   Turn off the Bunsen burner and allow the evaporation basin to cool for a few minutes.

7   Once the evaporating basin has cooled move the evaporating basin onto the heat-resistant mat. Allow the evaporating basin containing water sample A to cool further on the heat-resistant mat.

8   Repeat steps 2–7 with water sample B.

9   Make sure that both evaporating basins are dry. Reweigh each evaporating basin on the weighing scales. Record the final mass in the results table in the Recording data section.

Recording data

1 Record your results in the tables.

Melting and boiling point of water

	Temperature of melting ice / °C	Temperature of boiling water / °C
Water sample A		
Water sample B		

Testing for dissolved substances

	Mass of evaporating basin / g	Mass of evaporating basin with dissolved substances / g	Mass of dissolved substances / g
Water sample A			
Water sample B			

Handling data

2 Water has a melting point of 0 °C. Use your results to calculate the difference in melting point between each sample and pure water.

Water sample A had a temperature difference of .... °C from pure water.

Water sample B had a temperature difference of .... °C from pure water.

3 Water has a boiling point of 100 °C. Use your results to calculate the difference in boiling point between each sample and pure water.

Water sample A had a temperature difference of .... °C from pure water.

Water sample B had a temperature difference of .... °C from pure water.

4 Using your results for dissolved substances, estimate the mass of dissolved substances per dm^3 in each sample.

Water sample A has a mass of .... g/dm^3.

Water sample B has a mass of .... g/dm^3.

> **TIP**
>
> Remember you used 25 cm^3 of water samples so you will first need to calculate the mass of dissolved substances per cm^3.

Analysis

5   Based on your results, complete the table by adding a tick or a cross if there was evidence for each sample being pure water or not.

	Melting point	Boiling point	Dissolved substances
Water sample A			
Water sample B			

Evaluation

6   How could you have improved the accuracy of your data for melting and boiling point?

....

....

7   Suggest an improvement you could make to the method to improve the reliability of your data.

....

8   A control sample of water was not used in this investigation. Even though the melting point, boiling point and mass of dissolved substances for pure water are known, why would including a control sample of pure water have been useful?

....

....

....

EXAM-STYLE QUESTIONS

1   Two students are investigating the percentage of oxygen found in the air.
    They have left some wet iron wool in an inverted boiling tube (as shown in the
    diagram). One student is not sure that the reaction is complete and he thinks
    that there is still oxygen in the tube.

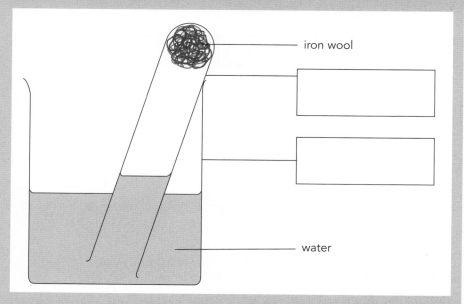

   a   What can he do to make sure the reaction has finished?

   ....

   .... **[1]**

   b   Complete the boxes to name the apparatus shown in the diagram.   **[2]**

CONTINUED

To get more accurate data, the students repeated the experiment using a different set of apparatus. This time they placed wet iron wool into a conical flask and attached the flask to a gas syringe open to $100\,cm^3$ to measure the decrease in volume.

c   Use the gas syringe diagrams below to complete the table of results and **calculate** the decrease in the volume of gas.

Repeat measurement	Gas syringe diagram	Volume / cm³	Decrease in volume / cm³
1	30 40 50 60 70 80 90 100		
2	30 40 50 60 70 80 90 100		
3	30 40 50 60 70 80 90 100		
4	30 40 50 60 70 80 90 100		

[8]

COMMAND WORD

calculate: work out from given facts, figures or information

d   Calculate the mean decrease in the volume of gas.

.... [2]

e   As a control experiment, the students attached the gas syringe to a conical flask containing dry iron wool and left it for three days. What do you think the decrease in volume of gas was?

.... [2]

[Total: 15]

2   The students are discussing the results of their investigation into the effect of acid rain on different metals. In their investigation, they used different metals and observed the effect of corrosion. Look at their results in the table.

Name of metal	Level of corrosion after 14 days
Silver	none
Lead	some corrosion
Aluminium	very corroded

CONTINUED

From the results, one student concludes that silver should be used as a building material in areas where there is a lot of acid rain. The second student disagrees and says she can think of two reasons why using silver as a building material is a bad idea.

a   **Suggest** two reasons the second student could use to support her argument.

....

....

.... [2]

b   **Consider**, from the results, which of the metals is most reactive.

.... [1]

c   **Predict** how much corrosion would be observed if the experiment was repeated using magnesium.

.... [1]

d   Suggest how you could measure the pH of the acid rain that was used.

....

.... [1]

COMMAND WORDS
suggest: apply knowledge and understanding to situations where there are a range of valid responses in order to make proposals/ put forward considerations
consider: review and respond to given information
predict: suggest what may happen based on available information

Many lakes are affected by acid rain and so the government is monitoring the pH of the lakes. Two students are sent a sample of water from a nearby lake to test using a pH meter. They recorded the pH of the samples sent every day for 14 days in a table:

Day	pH of sample
1	6.5
2	6.4
3	6.5
4	6.6
5	5.5
6	5.5
7	5.6
8	5.7
9	5.8
10	6.9
11	7.0
12	7.0
13	6.9
14	6.9

CONTINUED

e   Construct a graph to show the results of the experiment.

[5]

f   **Analyse** the results and your graph to show which day it rained.

....

.... [1]

As part of the work to prevent damage caused by acid rain, governments are adding lime to the lake to reduce the acidity.

g   Using the results and your graph, suggest which day lime was added to the lake and give a reason for your answer.   [2]

[Total: 13]

COMMAND WORD

analyse: examine in detail to show meaning, identify elements and the relationship between them

> Chapter 18

Introduction to organic chemistry

THE INVESTIGATIONS IN THIS CHAPTER WILL:

- enable you to describe hydrocarbons as saturated or unsaturated

- enable you to distinguish between saturated and unsaturated molecules by testing the compound using aqueous bromine

- enable you to distinguish different organic compounds by their molecular and displayed formulae

- compare a variety of organic compounds using their physical properties.

Practical investigation 18.1: Testing for saturated and unsaturated compounds

KEY WORDS

aqueous bromine: bromine dissolved in water

hydrocarbons: organic compounds which contain carbon and hydrogen only; the alkanes and alkenes are two series of hydrocarbons

saturated: an organic compound containing the maximum number of hydrogen atoms whilst also containing no double or triple bonds, e.g. alkanes

unsaturated: an organic compound that contains double or triple bonds between the carbon atoms, e.g. alkenes

IN THIS INVESTIGATION YOU WILL:

- identify saturated and unsaturated compounds using different chemical tests

- confirm conclusions based on multiple sources of evidence

- test a variety of common foodstuffs to identify if they contain saturated or unsaturated hydrocarbons.

YOU WILL NEED:

- test-tube rack • pipettes • eight test-tubes • eight rubber stoppers
- aqueous bromine (0.006 mol/dm³) • dilute acidified potassium manganate(VII)
- coconut oil (saturated hydrocarbon) • hexene (unsaturated hydrocarbon)
- unknown hydrocarbon samples A and B • safety glasses • lab coat • gloves.

Safety

- Wear eye protection throughout.

- Hexene is a moderate hazard, flammable and harmful for the aquatic environment. Waste from experiments using hexene must not be poured down the drain.

- Aqueous bromine is corrosive so wear gloves when handling it.

- Potassium manganate is an irritant, harmful if swallowed and can stain skin.

Getting started

In this investigation you will be examining saturated and unsaturated compounds.
In the space below draw an example of the structural formula of a saturated and an unsaturated hydrocarbon compound.

Saturated compound   **Unsaturated compound**

Method

Aqueous bromine test

1   Add 2 cm³ of coconut oil to one of the test-tubes.

2   Using a pipette, slowly add six drops of aqueous bromine to the test-tube. Close the test-tube with the rubber stopper and then shake it to mix the two liquids together. Record the colour in your table. (You will need to design your data collection table in the Recording data section.)

> **TIP**
>
> Do not use your thumb to cover the end of the test-tube, always use a rubber stopper.

3   Repeat steps 1 and 2 with hexene, sample A and sample B.

Dilute acidified potassium manganate(VII) test

1   Add $2\,cm^3$ of coconut oil to one of the test-tubes.

2   Using a pipette, slowly add six drops of dilute acidified potassium manganate(VII) to the test-tube. Close the test-tube with the rubber stopper and then shake the tube to mix the two liquids together. Record the colour in your table.

3   Repeat steps 1 and 2 with the hexene, sample A and sample B.

Recording data

1   Design a results table to record your data.

Analysis

2   Based on your result, determine which samples were saturated and which were unsaturated. Record your answers in the table.

Saturated hydrocarbons	Unsaturated hydrocarbons

3 Products made from animal fats usually contain saturated hydrocarbon chains, whereas products made from plants tend to contain unsaturated hydrocarbon chains. Predict the results for each type of product in the table below.

Product	Test result with aqueous bromine	Test result with dilute acidified potassium manganate(VII)
Milk		
Olive oil		
Sesame oil		
Cream		

Evaluation

4 Why was it useful to conduct more than one test for unsaturated compounds?

....

....

REFLECTION

Look back at the learning intentions for this investigation. Have you achieved all of them?

How do you know?

Do you feel confident in your ability to assess how well you have done in practical investigations?

Practical investigation 18.2: Chemical reactions of homologous series

KEY WORDS

homologous series: a family of similar compounds with similar chemical properties due to the presence of the same functional group

IN THIS INVESTIGATION YOU WILL:

- investigate the chemical properties of homologous series of organic compounds by performing qualitative chemical tests

- learn about alcohols and carboxylic acids.

> **YOU WILL NEED:**
>
> • test-tube rack • 12 test-tubes • test-tube holder • alcohols (methanol, ethanol, propan-1-ol) • carboxylic acids (methanoic acid, ethanoic acid, propanoic acid all at 1.0 mol/dm³) • 16 pipettes • Bunsen burner • gauze • tripod • heat-resistant mat • spatula • sodium hydrogen carbonate powder • sodium hydrogen carbonate solution (0.5 mol/dm³) • concentrated sulfuric acid (1.5 mol/dm³) • measuring cylinder • beaker (250 cm³) • distilled water • marker pen • safety glasses • lab coat • gloves.

Safety

• Wear eye protection throughout.

• Propanoic acid and concentrated sulfuric acid are corrosive.

• Methanol is toxic, a health hazard, and highly flammable.

• Ethanoic acid is an irritant.

• Ethanol is harmful if ingested and highly flammable.

• Propan-1-ol is corrosive, an irritant and highly flammable. Ask your teacher how to dispose of waste from experiments using propan-1-ol, do not pour waste down the drain.

• Make sure that you keep the flammable alcohols away from the Bunsen flame.

Getting started

In this investigation you will be comparing the chemical reactions of two different homologous series of compounds: alcohols and carboxylic acids. One of the tests you will be performing is reacting the alcohols and carboxylic acids with a base: sodium hydrogen carbonate. Use your knowledge of acids and bases to predict what will happened when alcohols and carboxylic acids are reacted with sodium hydrogen carbonate.

Method

Test 1

1 Use the marker pen to label six test-tubes with the names of the liquids you will be testing. Place the labelled test-tubes in the test-tube rack.

2 Use a pipette to add one drop of concentrated sulfuric acid to each of the six test-tubes.

3 Use a pipette to add 8–10 drops of ethanoic acid to each test-tube.

4 Use a pipette to add 8–10 drops of methanol to the first test-tube.

5 Use the measuring cylinder to add 100 cm³ of water to the 250 cm³ beaker. Carefully lower the tube into the beaker so that the tube stands upright but at a slight slant (in a position that is not vertical).

6   Set up the Bunsen burner, tripod and gauze on the heat-resistant mat well away from your test-tubes.

7   Heat the beaker on a cool blue flame, until the water begins to boil. Once the water is boiling, stop heating immediately. Turn off the Bunsen burner.

8   Let the test-tube rest in the hot water for approximately one minute. Observe the mixture in the test-tube carefully. If the mixture begins to boil, use the test-tube holder to lift the test-tube out of the water. Wait until the mixture stops boiling and then return the test-tube to the beaker.

9   After one minute, remove the test-tube and place the tube in the test-tube rack. Allow the test-tube to cool.

10   Half fill a test-tube with the sodium hydrogen carbonate solution.

11   Slowly pour the cooled mixture into the sodium hydrogen carbonate solution.

12   Use your hand to waft the odour from the mouth of the test-tube towards your nose.

> **TIP**
>
> You can waft the odour from the test-tube by waving your hand over the mouth of the test-tube.

13   Record your observation in the results table.

14   Repeat steps 4–13 with each of the liquids.

Test 2

1   Use the marker pen to label six test-tubes with the names of the liquids you will be testing. Place the labelled test-tubes in the test-tube rack.

2   Use a pipette to add $2\,cm^3$ of distilled water to each tube.

3   Using a clean pipette each time, add $2\,cm^3$ of methanol to the test-tube you have labelled 'methanol'.

4   Use a spatula to add a small amount of sodium hydrogen carbonate powder into the test-tube.

5   Record your observations in the results table.

6   Repeated steps 3–5 for each of the other liquids.

Recording data

1   Record your data in the table.

Liquid	Test 1 observations	Test 2 observations
Methanol		
Ethanol		
Propan-1-ol		

Methanoic acid		
Ethanoic acid		
Propanoic acid		

Analysis

2 Comment on any pattern that you saw in your results.

....

....

3 Homologous compounds display similar chemical properties to one another.
What evidence was provided by your investigation that suggests the alcohols you tested are
homologous compounds?

....

....

Evaluation

4 One of the observations you made in this investigation was smelling the product produced by
the reaction. Suggest why smelling compounds produced is rarely used in chemistry.

....

....

5 If butan-1-ol was tested using the same two tests in the methods you have just performed,
predict the results you would expect to observe.

Liquid	Test 1 observations	Test 2 observations
butan-1-ol		

6 Give a reason for each of the results you have predicted for butan-1-ol.

Test 1: ....

Test 2: ....

EXAM-STYLE QUESTIONS

1 As part of a healthy lifestyle, people are advised to cut down on saturated fats and increase their intake of unsaturated fats. You are given five different food spreads and you must design an investigation that would enable you to determine which ones contain unsaturated hydrocarbons. Remember to include safety precautions.

....

....

....

....

....

....

....

....

.... [7]

2 Some students were testing different liquids to sort them into a homologous series.

a One of the types of compound being tested was alkanes. Alkanes are saturated compounds.

   i **Define** the term *saturated*.

   ....

   .... [1]

   One of the other types of compound being tested was carboxylic acids.

   ii **Suggest** a test to identify an acid.

   ....

   .... [1]

COMMAND WORDS

define: give precise meaning

suggest: apply knowledge and understanding to situations where there are a range of valid responses in order to make proposals / put forward considerations

The students recorded their results in a table.

b   Add the name of the test for saturated/unsaturated compounds to their table.

Compound	pH	Test for saturated/ unsaturated compounds: .... [1]	Temperature / °C
1	4	Does not decolourise	25
2	7	Does not decolourise	26
3	7	Does not decolourise	25
4	5	Does not decolourise	26
5	7	Decolourises	24

c   From the results suggest which of the compounds were:

i   carboxylic acids

.... [1]

ii   alkanes

.... [1]

iii   alkenes

.... [1]

d   **Explain** why the temperature was not a useful measurement to take when trying to group compounds into different homologous series.

....

....

.... [2]

[Total: 8]

COMMAND WORD

explain: set out purposes or reasons / make the relationships between things evident / provide why and/or how and support with relevant evidence

Chapter 19

Reactions of organic compounds

THE INVESTIGATIONS IN THIS CHAPTER WILL:

- produce ethanol by fermentation using glucose and yeast

- enable you to describe the reaction of a carboxylic acid and an alcohol to form an ester

- enable you to describe the manufacture of alkenes and of hydrogen by cracking.

KEY WORDS

fermentation: a reaction carried out using a living organism, usually a yeast or bacteria, to produce a useful chemical compound; most usually refers to the production of ethanol

respiration: the chemical reaction (a combustion reaction) by which biological cells release the energy stored in glucose for use by the cell or the body; the reaction is exothermic and produces carbon dioxide and water as the chemical by-products

Practical investigation 19.1: The manufacture of ethanol by fermentation

IN THIS INVESTIGATION YOU WILL:

- use yeast to produce ethanol and carbon dioxide from glucose

- test different conditions to see which condition is the most suitable for fermentation.

YOU WILL NEED:

- boiling tube • spatula • glucose solution $(100\,g/dm^3)$ • yeast • oil
- measuring cylinder $(50\,cm^3)$ • stopper and delivery tube • two test-tubes
- water-bath/beaker of warm water $(40\,°C)$ • test-tube rack • test-tube holder
- limewater • safety glasses • lab coat • gloves.

Safety

• Wear eye protection throughout.

• Limewater is a moderate hazard.

Getting started

In this investigation you will need to carefully pour oil slowly into a test-tube. Practise pouring oil very slowly into a test-tube. Make sure you are able to start and stop pouring the oil precisely.

Method

1   Add $20\,cm^3$ of glucose solution to the boiling tube. Add two heaped spatulas of yeast to the tube. Carefully add $0.5\,cm^3$ of oil to the boiling tube so that it forms a thin layer on top of the mixture (Figure 19.1) and close the boiling tube using the stopper.

> **TIP**
>
> The oil will take time to flow down the side of the test-tube so pour a little oil at a time to prevent pouring too much in.

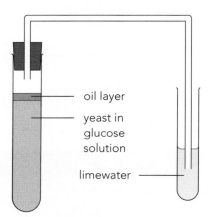

oil layer

yeast in glucose solution

limewater

Figure 19.1: Setup to ferment glucose.

2   Half fill two test-tubes with limewater and place the tubes in the test-tube rack.

3   Place the boiling tube into the water-bath or beaker of warm water. Place the end of the delivery tube so that it is submerged in one of the test-tubes with limewater. Bubbles should start to come out of the delivery tube.

4   After 40 minutes, observe the two tubes with limewater and record your results. You will need to design your data collection table in the Recording data section.

Recording data

1   Design a table to record your results.

Analysis

2   Use the words below to complete the sentences.

bread   **carbon dioxide**   **glucose**   **respiration**   **yeast**

Fermentation is a process where .... is turned into ethanol and

.... by the microorganism called .... This occurs when yeast

undergoes .... Fermentation is used in the production of ....

3   What do the limewater results show the presence of?

....

4   In this investigation you have looked at the by-product of fermentation as evidence for the process of fermentation taking place. The main purpose of using fermentation is the production of ethanol. Describe how you could use the chemical process of combustion to test for the presence of ethanol.

....

....

....

....

Evaluation

5   What was the purpose of the test-tube of limewater that did not contain the delivery tube?

....

....

6   Why was a layer of oil added to the mixture?

....

Practical investigation 19.2: Making esters from alcohols and acids

IN THIS INVESTIGATION YOU WILL:

〉 explore the reaction of carboxylic acids with alcohols

〉 learn how to name an ester by combining the names of the acid and alcohol that are used

〉 record observations based on odours (smells) produced by the esters you have made.

YOU WILL NEED:

- six test-tubes • pipettes • beaker (250 cm³) • test-tube rack • Bunsen burner
- heat-resistant mat • tripod and gauze • test-tube holder
- measuring cylinder (50 cm³) • timer/stopwatch • sodium hydrogen carbonate solution (0.5 mol/dm³) • ethanoic acid (1.0 mol/dm³) • propanoic acid (1.0 mol/dm³)
- concentrated sulfuric acid (1.5 mol/dm³) • three alcohols from: methanol, ethanol, propan-1-ol, butan-1-ol, butan-2-ol, propan-2-ol • safety glasses • lab coat • gloves.

Safety

- Wear eye protection throughout.

- Propanoic acid and concentrated sulfuric acid are corrosive.

- Ethanoic acid is an irritant.

- Methanol is toxic, a health hazard, and highly flammable.

- Ethanol is harmful if ingested and highly flammable.

- Propan-1-ol, propan-2-ol and butan-1-ol are corrosive, irritants and highly flammable.

- Butan-2-ol is flammable and an irritant.

- Make sure that you keep the flammable alcohols away from the Bunsen flame. Ask your teacher how to dispose of waste from experiments using alcohols, do not pour waste down the drain.

Getting started

You will be using a number of different alcohols in this experiment. In the space below, draw the display formula of methanol, ethanol and propan-1-ol.

> **TIP**
>
> The displayed formula of an organic molecule shows how the atoms and bonds in a molecule are arranged in space: all the atoms and covalent bonds must be shown.

Methanol   **Ethanol**   **Propan-1-ol**

Method

You will need to decide on three different combinations of acids (ethanoic or propanoic) and alcohols (methanol, ethanol, propan-1-ol, propan-2-ol, butan-1-ol or butan-2-ol). Add the details of the acids and alcohols into the results table in the Recording data section now.

1   Add one drop of concentrated sulfuric acid to each of four test-tubes (if this has not already been done for you).

2   Add 8–10 drops of ethanoic acid or propanoic acid to the sulfuric acid in the first test-tube.

3   Using a pipette, add 8–10 drops of your chosen alcohol to the first test-tube.

4   Use the measuring cylinder to add $50\,cm^3$ of water to the $250\,cm^3$ beaker. Carefully lower the tube into the beaker so that the tube stands upright but at a slight slant (in a position that is not vertical).

5   Set up the Bunsen burner, tripod and gauze on the heat-resistant mat well away from your test-tube.

6   On a cool blue flame, heat the beaker until the water begins to boil. Once the water is boiling, stop heating immediately. Turn off the Bunsen burner.

7   Let the test-tube rest in the hot water for approximately one minute. Observe the mixture in the test-tube carefully. If the mixture begins to boil, use the test-tube holder to lift the test-tube out of the water. Wait until the mixture stops boiling and then return the test-tube to the beaker.

8   After one minute has passed, remove the test-tube and place the tube in the test-tube rack. Allow the test-tube to cool.

9   Half fill a test-tube with the sodium hydrogen carbonate solution.

10 Slowly pour the cooled mixture into the sodium hydrogen carbonate solution.

> **TIP**
>
> Pour the liquids from tube to tube a few times to ensure that the liquids are well mixed.

11 Once you stop mixing, you should be able to see a layer forming on the top. This layer is the ester.

12 Use your hand to waft the odour from the mouth of the test-tube towards your nose. Record your observations in the results table.

13 Repeat steps 2–12 with each combination of acid and alcohol you have chosen to use.

Recording data

1   Complete the results table.

Test-tube	Acid used	Alcohol used	Smell produced
1			
2			
3			

Analysis

The first word in the name of an ester comes from the alcohol used.

Alcohol name	Ester name first word
Methanol	Methyl
Ethanol	Ethyl
Propanol	Propyl
Butanol	Butyl

The second word in the name of the ester comes from the acid used.

Acid name	Ester name second word
Ethanoic	Ethanoate
Propanoic	Propanoate

2   Using the information in the tables, suggest the names of the esters that you made.

   a   Test-tube 1 ....

   b   Test-tube 2 ....

   c   Test-tube 3 ....

3   Which alcohol and acid combination would need to be used to make the ester butyl ethanoate?

   ....

Evaluation

4   It is very likely that the first step of this experiment will have been done for you.
   Suggest why this might have been.

   ....

   ....

REFLECTION

Think about the different steps you performed in this investigation. Which particular steps did you find easy or difficult?

Are you confident when performing multi-step experiments with many repeats?

How could you improve your skills and organisation?

Practical investigation 19.3: Cracking hydrocarbons

KEY WORDS

catalytic cracking: the decomposition of long-chain alkanes into alkenes and alkanes of lower relative molecular mass; involves passing the larger alkane molecules over a catalyst heated to 500 °C

IN THIS INVESTIGATION YOU WILL:

- perform a small-scale version of the industrial process known as cracking

- break longer chain hydrocarbons into shorter chain hydrocarbons by carefully following a complex method

- learn about the conditions needed for cracking to take place successfully.

YOU WILL NEED:

- three test-tubes with rubber stoppers • test-tube rack • boiling tube
- stopper with hole to fit boiling tube and delivery tube • clamp stand with boss and clamp
- water trough or large beaker • delivery tube with Bunsen valve fitted
- Bunsen burner • heat-resistant mat • liquid paraffin • porcelain crushed into 0.5 cm fragments • mineral wool • aqueous bromine (0.01 mol/dm³)
- wooden splint • pipette • glass rod • safety glasses • lab coat • gloves.

Safety

- Wear eye protection throughout.

- Be very careful with the hot glassware.

- Paraffin is harmful if ingested and highly flammable.

- Make sure that you keep heating the boiling tube – if you stop heating, there is the possibility that water will be sucked back into the delivery tube. This is very dangerous and can cause the tube to shatter. If you see water being sucked back into the tube, loosen the boss on the clamp stand and lift the whole apparatus up higher so that the delivery tube is no longer in the water.

- Aqueous bromine is corrosive so wear gloves when handling it.

Getting started

You will be using a delivery tube with a Bunsen valve as there is danger that water can be sucked back into the test-tube if heating stops. For safety, practise loosening the boss so that you can lift the apparatus out of the water. Make sure you are able to do this confidently before you begin the practical.

Method

1   Add mineral wool to the boiling tube and press the wool down to the bottom of the tube using the glass rod. The mineral wool needs to be between 2 cm and 3 cm from the bottom of the tube.

2   Using the pipette, add 2 cm³ of liquid paraffin to the mineral wool.

3   Clamp the boiling tube near the mouth of the tube and then rotate the tube so that it is horizontal. Tighten the boss so that the tube is held securely in place (Figure 19.2).

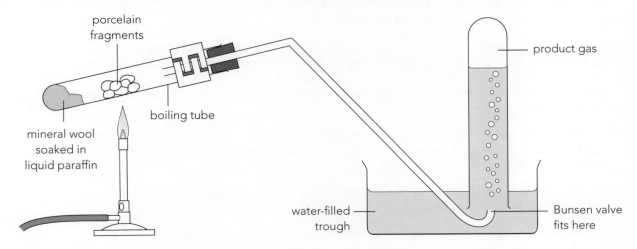

Figure 19.2: Setup for the cracking of hydrocarbons.

4   Carefully add some of the crushed porcelain fragments to the tube and push them to the middle of the tube using the glass rod. Loosen the boss and gently rotate the boiling tube so that there is a slight downward tilt towards the mineral wool. Retighten the boss.

5   Attach the delivery tube to the rubber stopper with the hole and then place the stopper securely on the mouth of the boiling tube. Make sure that there is a Bunsen valve fitted (Figure 19.3) to the delivery tube.

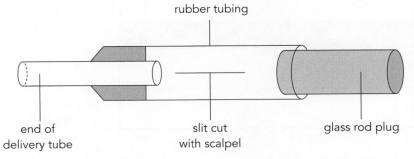

Figure 19.3: A Bunsen valve.

TIP
A Bunsen valve is a one-way valve used to avoid the problem of suck back.

6   Half fill the trough or beaker with water. Fill the test-tubes with water and then place your thumb over the end of the tube. Invert the tubes and then place them upside down in the trough or beaker.

7   Add the test-tube stoppers to the trough or beaker and make sure the narrow ends of the stoppers are pointing upwards so that you can easily push the test-tubes down on to them. This will allow you to close the test-tubes under water and stop any gases from escaping.

8   Place the end of delivery tube attached to the Bunsen valve in the water trough or beaker so that the tube is well submerged. When you heat the boiling tube, gas will come out of the valve. The gas will be collected in the inverted test-tubes.

9   Light the Bunsen burner and adjust the collar to give a gentle blue flame. Heat the porcelain fragments until the fragments begin to glow slightly red. At this point you can start to heat the mineral wool. You will need to move the Bunsen burner back and forth between the porcelain fragments and mineral wool. Avoid heating near the rubber stopper as it may catch fire and will produce harmful fumes.

10   Bubbles will start to come from the valve in the water. Use the test-tube to collect the gas. Once the tube is full of gas, close the tube with a stopper from the bottom of the beaker/trough and place it in the test-tube rack.

11   Once all of the tubes are full, lift the delivery tube out of the water. Only at this point will it be safe to stop heating the boiling tube.

12   Open the first test-tube and carefully waft the contents of the tube so that you may smell the odour. Record your observations in the results table below.

13   Use the pipette to add a few drops of aqueous bromine to the second tube. Shake the tube and record your observations.

14   Light a wooden split and open the third tube. Place the wooden splint near the mouth of the tube. Record your observations.

Recording data

1   Complete the results table.

Tube	Observation
1 smell	
2 aqueous bromine	
3 lighted splint	

Analysis

2   With reference to your results, draw a conclusion about the gas in the test-tubes.

....

....

> **TIP**
>
> Shorter-chain hydrocarbons burn with a characteristic yellow flame and have a
> distinctive smell.

Evaluation

3   Gas was produced when the porcelain fragments were being heated. This was before the mineral
wool was heated. Why were bubbles coming out of the valve?

....

....

4   Why was it necessary to heat the boiling tube for the duration of the experiment?

....

....

5   Why were the porcelain fragments used?

....

6   Why were the porcelain fragments heated?

....

> **REFLECTION**
>
> Think about the safety precautions you have taken in this and other investigations. Do you
> understand how specific safety precautions relate to different parts of an experiment?
>
> Are you able to apply your knowledge of safety aspects to the design and planning
> of investigations?

EXAM-STYLE QUESTIONS

1   Two students were using yeast to ferment glucose.

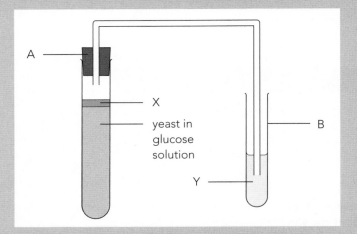

a   **Identify** the apparatus labelled A and B in the diagram.

A   ....

B   ....   [2]

b   Identify liquid X and **suggest** the purpose of it in this experiment.

....

....

.... [2]

c   Identify liquid Y and suggest the purpose of it in this experiment.

....

....

.... [2]

d   The students heated the boiling tube with the yeast and glucose solution
to 80 °C for three minutes. **Predict** and **explain** the result you would expect
to see in the liquid marked Y.

....

....

.... [4]

[Total: 10]

COMMAND WORDS

identify: name/ select/recognise

suggest: apply knowledge and understanding to situations where there are a range of valid responses in order to make proposals / put forward considerations

COMMAND WORDS

predict: suggest what may happen based on available information

explain: set out purposes or reasons / make the relationships between things evident / provide why and/or how and support with relevant evidence

CONTINUED

2 Two students were trying to crack a sample of long-chain hydrocarbons into shorter-chain hydrocarbons.

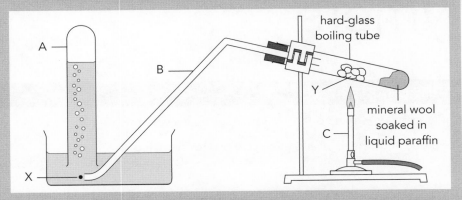

a Identify the apparatus in the diagram.

A ....

B ....

C .... [3]

b i **State** the name of the piece of apparatus labelled as Y in the diagram.

.... [1]

ii Suggest the purpose of this piece of apparatus.

.... [1]

c This experiment has not been set up safely. **Evaluate**, with specific reference to the part of the diagram labelled X, why this is a dangerous way to complete this practical.

....

.... [2]

d **Describe** how you could test for the presence of alkenes in the gas produced by cracking.

....

.... [2]

[Total: 9]

COMMAND WORDS

state: express in clear terms

evaluate: judge or calculate the quality, importance, amount, or value of something

describe: state the points of a topic / give characteristics and main features

> Chapter 20

Petrochemicals and polymers

THE INVESTIGATIONS IN THIS CHAPTER WILL:

- compare the usefulness of fuels by determining the energy they release when burned

- compare the physical properties of polymers and the implications for recycling.

Practical investigation 20.1: Comparing fuels

KEY WORDS

biofuel: fuels made directly from the products of living matter, e.g. ethanol

fossil fuels: fuels, such as coal, oil and natural gas, formed underground over geological periods of time from the remains of plants and animals

fuel: a substance that can be used as a source of energy, usually by burning (combustion)

plastics: polymers that can be moulded or shaped by the action of heat and pressure

polymer: a substance consisting of very large molecules made by polymerising a large number of repeating units or monomers

IN THIS INVESTIGATION YOU WILL:

- design a method to compare the amount of energy in different types of fuel by making careful measurements of temperature changes

- ensure that your method is valid by selecting appropriate independent and dependent variables.

YOU WILL NEED:

- clamp and stand • heat-resistant mat • thermometer • measuring cylinder (100 cm³)
- pipette • boiling tube • crucible • paraffin • ethanol • safety glasses
- lab coat • gloves • balance.

Safety

- Wear eye protection throughout.
- Ethanol and paraffin harmful if ingested and highly flammable.

Getting started

Think about what you know about the production and chemistry of paraffin (kerosene) and ethanol, and how these can be used as fuels. Discuss with your partner which of the two fuels you think will have the most energy.

Method

1   Design a method to compare the energy contained in paraffin and ethanol, using the equipment list given.

My independent variable is ....

My dependent variable is ....

My control variables will be ...., ..., ...

I will make my results accurate by:

....

....

I will make my results reliable by:

....

....

This is how I will set up my apparatus:

To make sure I work safely, I will:

....

....

My method will be:

....

....

....

....

....

....

....

....

....

TIP
Make sure you include all of the apparatus in your method.

See the Practical skills and support section at the start of this workbook for more information about accuracy/reliability and designing an experiment.

Once you have written your method, get your teacher to check your method before you begin the experiment.

Recording data

2 Design a results table to record your results.

Analysis

3 Write a conclusion for your experiment to explain which of the two fuels contained more energy. Make sure that you include references to the actual experimental data.

....

....

....

....

Evaluation

4 Only some of the heat energy from the burning fuel was used to heat the water. Where did the rest of the heat energy go?

....

....

5 How could you have improved your experiment so that less of this heat energy was lost?

....

....

6 Can you explain why many people are reluctant to stop using fossil fuels even when there are alternatives available?

....

....

....

....

REFLECTION

Imagine you are trying to persuade someone to switch to using biofuels. Based on what you have learnt in this practical investigation, what arguments would you use?

What other features of fossil fuels and biofuels could you also refer to in your argument?

....

....

Practical investigation 20.2: Comparing the physical properties of polymers and the implications for recycling

IN THIS INVESTIGATION YOU WILL:

- identify different types of polymers based on their physical properties so that they can be sorted for recycling

- use buoyancy in different liquids to determine the density of unknown samples of polymers.

YOU WILL NEED:

- five boiling tubes • test-tube rack • permanent marker • glass rod
- samples of four different plastics (five pieces of each) • liquids 1–5
- measuring cylinder (50 cm³ or 100 cm³) • safety glasses • lab coat • gloves.

Safety

- Wear eye protection throughout.
- Ethanol (which will be in tubes 1 and 2) harmful if ingested and highly flammable.
- Potassium carbonate (which will be in tubes 4 and 5) is an irritant.

Getting started

This practical will focus on the property of density to distinguish between different polymers so that the polymers can be identified for recycling. Discuss what you understand about the terms *polymer*, *plastics* and *density* with your partner.

Method

1   Label the boiling tubes 1–5 and place them in the labelled holes in the test-tube rack.

2   Add $20\,cm^3$ of one of the five liquids to the matching numbered boiling tube.

3   Add a sample of each plastic to each of the tubes.

4   Using the glass rod, stir the liquid in each boiling tube.

> **TIP**
>
> Remember to wash the measuring cylinder between each liquid and to wash the glass rod after stirring each tube to avoid contaminating the liquids and affecting their density.

5   Look at each boiling tube and record whether the samples of plastic float or sink. Record the data in the table below.

Recording data

1   For each sample, record whether it sank or floated in each liquid by writing 'S' (sank) or 'F' (floated).

Sample	Tube				
	1	2	3	4	5
1					
2					
3					
4					

Handling data

2   Based on the results and the data given in Tables 20.1 and 20.2, determine the density range of each polymer.

Liquid	Density / g per cm³
1	0.91
2	0.94
3	1.00
4	1.15
5	1.38

Table 20.1: Liquid density chart.

Polymer name	Density range / g per cm³
polypropylene	0.89–0.91
low-density polyethylene	0.91–0.93
high-density polyethylene	0.94–0.96
polystyrene	1.04–1.12
polyvinyl chloride (PVC)	1.20–1.55
polyethylene terephthalate (PET)	1.38–1.41

Table 20.2: Polymer density chart.

Sample	Density range / g per cm³
1	
2	
3	
4	

Analysis

3   Complete the following sentences to identify each type of polymer:

Sample 1 was .... because it was more dense than liquid ....
but less dense than liquid ....

Sample 2 was .... because it was more dense than liquid ....
but less dense than liquid ....

Sample 3 was .... because it was more dense than liquid ....
but less dense than liquid ....

Sample 4 was .... because it was more dense than liquid ....
but less dense than liquid ....

4   List the polymers from the least to the most dense based on your results.

....

....

....

....

Evaluation

5   Why might there be some errors in your results?

....

....

6   Polymer X has a density of 0.98 g/cm^3. Predict the results you would obtain if polymer X was
placed into the same five liquids used in your investigation. Write 'S' for sink or 'F' for float.

Tube	1	2	3	4	5
X					

7   Most polymer products are labelled with recycling information, but some are not. This causes
problems when it comes to recycling the polymer products. Suggest how a plastic recycling
facility could use your findings about polymer density to identify different polymers.

....

....

....

....

REFLECTION

There are many areas where your learning of chemistry will overlap with other sciences, e.g. density is a physical property of a material and you are likely to have first encountered the term in an earlier physics course. Which areas of chemistry can you think of that overlap with your other courses?

How does your knowledge of chemistry help your learning in other courses and vice versa?

....

....

EXAM-STYLE QUESTIONS

1   Two students were comparing two fuels to see which one contained more energy. They set up the apparatus shown in the diagram. They were comparing methanol and paraffin.

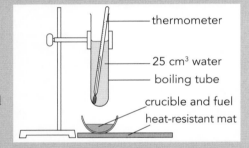

The two students used the methanol first. They measured $1\,cm^3$ of the fuel and placed it in the crucible. They then added $25\,cm^3$ of water to the boiling tube. They measured the temperature of the water and then lit the fuel. After the fuel had finished burning, they measured the temperature again.

a   **Calculate** the temperature change for each repeat for methanol using the thermometer readings in the table.

COMMAND WORD

calculate: work out from given facts, figures or information

Repeat number	Thermometer at start / °C	Thermometer at finish / °C	Temperature change / °C
1			
2			

CONTINUED

Repeat number	Thermometer at start / °C	Thermometer at finish / °C	Temperature change / °C
3	30 / 25 / 20	30 / 25 / 20	

[3]

The pair then did the experiment again, but this time they used paraffin.

b Calculate the temperature change for each repeat for paraffin using the thermometer readings in the table.

Repeat number	Thermometer at start / °C	Thermometer at finish / °C	Temperature change / °C
1	30 / 25 / 20	60 / 55 / 50	
2	30 / 25 / 20	50 / 45 / 40	
3	30 / 25 / 20	60 / 55 / 50	

[3]

c Calculate the mean temperature change for each fuel.

Mean temperature change for methanol = ... °C

Mean temperature change for paraffin = ... °C   [2]

CONTINUED

COMMAND WORD

compare: identify/ comment on similarities and/or differences

d Plot a bar graph to **compare** the average temperature change for the two fuels.

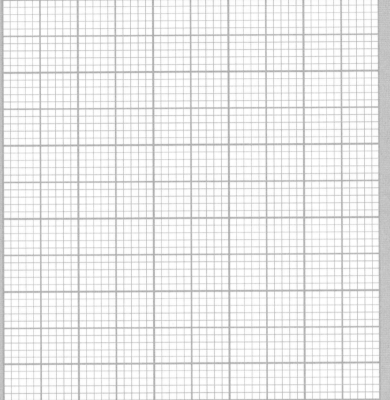

[4]
[Total: 12]

COMMAND WORD

define: give precise meaning

2 Two students are investigating some unknown samples of polymers.

a **Define** the term *polymer*.

....

.... [1]

The students had four different types of polymers that had been cut into strips. Each strip was weighed. Each of the polymer strips were then added to test-tubes containing either concentrated sulfuric acid or concentrated sodium hydroxide. After 15 minutes the strips were removed, washed with distilled water and allowed to dry. The polymer strips were then reweighed.

CONTINUED

The results of the experiment are below.

b   Calculate the change in mass for each polymer.

Polymer	Mass of strip before being placed in concentrated sulfuric acid / g	Mass of strip after being placed in concentrated sulfuric acid / g	Change in mass / g
W	0.425	0.400	
X	0.565	0.565	
Y	0.455	0.385	
Z	0.535	0.535	

Polymer	Mass of strip before being placed in concentrated sodium hydroxide / g	Mass of strip after being placed in concentrated sodium hydroxide / g	Change in mass / g
W	0.410	0.410	
X	0.460	0.395	
Y	0.525	0.525	
Z	0.335	0.275	

[4]

c   Use the data in the results table to **suggest** which of the polymers could be used to:

   i   make a bottle to contain hydrochloric acid

.... [2]

   ii   make a pipe to transport ammonia solution

.... [2]

d   The monomers that form polymers come from the fractional distillation of petroleum. **State** which property of the fractions of petroleum is used to separate the fractions during fractional distillation.

.... [1]

[Total: 10]

COMMAND WORDS

suggest: apply knowledge and understanding to situations where there are a range of valid responses in order to make proposals/ put forward considerations

state: express in clear terms

> Chapter 21
Experimental design and separation techniques

THE INVESTIGATIONS IN THIS CHAPTER WILL:

- explore suitable methods for separating a mixture of substances

- use a variety of different apparatus safely and appropriately

- explore a variety of different separation techniques and the appropriate conditions under which to use each technique

- use chromatography to analyse the composition of solutions.

Practical investigation 21.1:
Filtration, distillation and evaporation

KEY WORDS

distillation: the process of boiling a liquid and then condensing the vapour produced, back into a liquid: used to purify liquids and to separate liquids from solutions

evaporation: a process occurring at the surface of a liquid, involving the change of state from a liquid into a vapour at a temperature below the boiling point

filtration: the separation of a solid from a liquid, using a fine filter paper that does not allow the solid to pass through

insoluble: term that describes a substance that does not dissolve in a particular solvent

soluble: term that describes a solute that dissolves in a particular solvent

solute: the solid substance that has dissolved in a liquid (the solvent) to form a solution

solvent: the liquid that dissolves the solid solute to form a solution; water is the most common solvent but liquids in organic chemistry that can act as solvents are called *organic solvents*

IN THIS INVESTIGATION YOU WILL:

- separate dissolved solids from solvents to collect either the solvent or the solute

- choose the appropriate apparatus and method when given information about the product needed.

YOU WILL NEED:

- filter paper • clamp stand with clamp and boss • funnel • spatula
- two beakers (250 cm³) • magnet • small plastic bag
- boiling tube with stopper and delivery tube or Liebig condenser (if available) • ice
- evaporating basin • Bunsen burner • tripod • gauze • boiling tube
- sample to be separated (sand, salt, iron filings and 150 cm³ of water) • safety glasses
- lab coat • gloves.

Safety

- Wear eye protection throughout.

- You will need to stand for the practical because hot liquids are being used.

- Remember to take care when handling hot glassware and also to be careful when the water is boiling as the steam will be very hot.

Getting started

For each of the combinations below, state the most suitable technique for separating the substances.

a   To obtain salt from a salt solution

....

b   To obtain iron filings from sand

....

c   To obtain water from a salt solution

....

d   To obtain iron filings and sand from a water suspension

....

See Chapter 21 in the Coursebook for more information on separating and purifying substances.

Method

1 **a** The aim of the investigation is to obtain salt, sand and iron filings from the mixture. Think about the order in which you will need to use each of the techniques you described in the Getting started section. Write the sequence of techniques in order below.

> **TIP**
>
> Think about the things that each technique separates. Put the steps in order to separate the mixtures in the most effective way. Start by thinking about solubility.

  i ....

  ii ....

  iii ....

  iv ....

b Design a short method to explain how you will use filtration to separate the insoluble solids from the liquid.

Separating insoluble solids from liquids by filtration

  i ....

  ii ....

  iii ....

  iv ....

  v ....

> **TIP**
>
> The substance that remains after evaporation, distillation or filtration is known as the residue. The liquid or solution that has passed through a filter is known as the filtrate.

2 For this section you will need to split the filtrate you have obtained into two samples: one sample each for use in the two remaining techniques. Design the methods you would use.

Separating water from a solution that contains a dissolved solid

a **i** ....

  ii ....

  iii ....

  iv ....

  v ....

Separating a soluble solid from water to obtain the solid

b   i   ....

    ii   ....

    iii   ....

    iv   ....

    v   ....

Separating two solids from each other

c   i   ....

    ii   ....

    iii   ....

Get your teacher to check your methods before you begin the experiment.

Evaluation

3   How could you have tested the original sample to confirm the presence of water?

....

....

4   How could you test the purified water to make sure that there was no salt in the water?
(Remember that you are not allowed to taste anything in a laboratory.)

....

....

REFLECTION

Think about the apparatus you have used in this investigation and your other chemistry practicals. Do you understand why each piece of equipment was used?

Are you confident in safely using the different pieces of equipment?

Which apparatus do you have difficulty using?

Practical investigation 21.2: Chromatography

KEY WORD

chromatography: a technique employed for the separation of mixtures of dissolved substances, which was originally used to separate coloured dyes

IN THIS INVESTIGATION YOU WILL:

- separate dissolved solids from solutions obtained from different coloured sweets

- identify different dissolved solids by interpreting chromatograms

⟩ use R_f values to compare spots on a chromatogram.

YOU WILL NEED:

- beaker (250 cm³) • chromatography paper/filter paper
- samples of three different coloured sweets • paper clip • small paintbrush
- wooden splint • safety glasses • lab coat • gloves.

Safety

- Wear eye protection throughout.

- Food dye can stain the skin and clothing.

- Do not eat any of the sweets.

Getting started

You will need to be able to use R_f values to compare different spots on the chromatograms. This is very simple to do as all that is needed is a simple mathematical division.
The distance travelled by each spot is divided by the distance travelled by the solvent. The ratio of these distances is the R_f value.

$$R_f \text{ value} = \frac{\text{distance travelled by the spot}}{\text{distance travelled by the solvent}}$$

Practise calculating R_f values for the examples shown below. Give your answers to two decimal places.

Spot	Distance travelled by spot / mm	Distance travelled by solvent / mm	R_f value
X	55	82	
Y	23	57	
Z	19	44	

Method

1   Take the filter paper and, using a ruler, measure 2 cm from the bottom of the paper. Use a pencil to draw a baseline across the paper from one side to the other side.

2   At 2 cm intervals label the baseline with the name of the colour of each coloured sweet that will be used. Make sure you use a pencil to write the label.

> **TIP**
>
> You might want to use a key for each colour instead of writing out the whole name of each colour.

3   Dip the paintbrush in water and rub the tip of the wet brush on the first coloured sweet. The dye on the surface of the sweet should dissolve in the water on the paintbrush.

4   Lightly touch the tip of the paintbrush onto the filter paper next to where you have written the colour's label. Repeat this several times until you have a small concentrated spot of colour.

5   Clean the paintbrush and then repeat steps 3 and 4 for each of the other colours of sweets.

6   Fold the top of the filter paper over the wooden splint and use the paper clip to hold the filter paper in place. Place the filter paper and splint in the empty beaker to test the height. The bottom of the filter paper should be just touching the bottom of the beaker. If the filter paper is too long you can either cut the paper to size or fold more of the paper over the wooden splint.

7   Add water to the beaker until the water is just below the baseline that you have drawn on the filter paper.

8   When the ink has climbed about three-quarters of the way up the paper, remove the filter paper and allow the filter paper to dry.

Recording data

1   For each sample of coloured sweet, you will need to measure the distance travelled by each of the spots. To do this you will need to use your origin as a starting point and then measure the distance to the middle of each spot and also the total distance travelled by the solvent (water) (Figure 21.1).

Total distance travelled by solvent: ....mm. This is known as the solvent front.

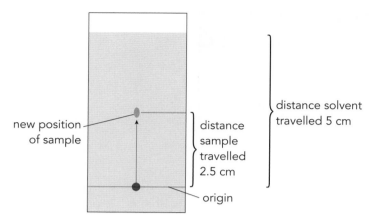

Figure 21.1: How to measure the distance travelled by a sample and the distance travelled by a solvent.

2   Complete the data tables.

TIP
You may not need all of the rows in each table as this will depend on the number of different dyes contained in each sample.

Sample 1 (sweet colour: ....)

Spot number	Distance travelled by spot/mm

Sample 2 (sweet colour: ....)

Spot number	Distance travelled by spot/mm

Sample 3 (sweet colour: ....)

Spot number	Distance travelled by spot/mm

Handling data

3 To allow comparison of different spots, you need to calculate the R_f value for each of the spots. Complete the tables below.

Sample 1

Spot number	R_f value

Sample 2

Spot number	R_f value

Sample 3

Spot number	R_f value

Analysis

4 With reference to the R_f values, identify if any spot numbers in the samples were the same.

....

....

....

5 Was there a dissolved substance that was found in only one sample? Describe this with reference to the R_f value.

....

....

....

Evaluation

6 Identify a source of error in the investigation and how you would change the experiment to solve this problem.

....

....

REFLECTION

You are often asked to identify sources of error in an investigation.

Think about what you know about sources of error and how these can affect the results of an investigation.

Are you confident in evaluating experimental methods and suggesting possible improvements?

EXAM-STYLE QUESTIONS

1   Sweets often come in bright colours so that they appear attractive.
These colours are made using water-soluble food dyes, which can be
separated using the apparatus shown in the diagram.

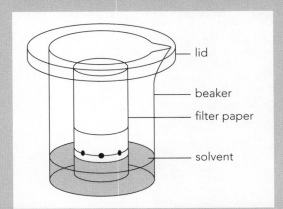

a   What name is given to this separation technique?

.... [1]

b   **Suggest** a suitable solvent.

.... [1]

c   What would you use to draw the line at the bottom of the paper?

.... [1]

d   What is the name given to this line?

.... [1]

Look at the diagram. Three types of food dye A–C were placed on the
paper alongside the results for two types of sweets D and E.

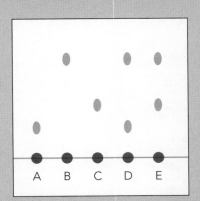

COMMAND WORD

suggest: apply
knowledge and
understanding
to situations
where there are
a range of valid
responses in order
to make proposals/
put forward
considerations

CONTINUED

    e **i**   Suggest which dyes were used to make sweet D.

                 .... **[2]**

        ii   Suggest which dyes were used to make sweet E.

                 .... **[2]**

                                                                         [Total: 8]

2   A mixture of two liquids with similar boiling points is separated using a method called fractional distillation. The diagram shows how apparatus can be arranged to carry out this type of separation.

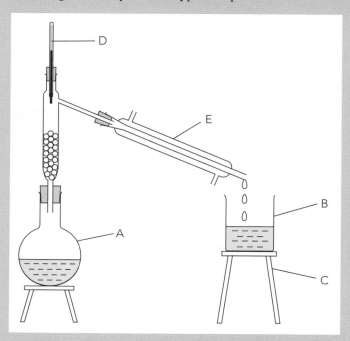

    a   Name the apparatus used.

        A ....   D ....

        B ....   E ....

        C ....   **[5]**

    b   Draw an arrow to show the direction that water would flow through the cooling apparatus.   **[1]**

    c   Label where heat would be added to the apparatus in order to cause the mixture of liquids to boil.   **[1]**

                                                                         [Total: 7]

Chapter 22

Chemical analysis

THE INVESTIGATIONS IN THIS CHAPTER WILL:

- show how the colours produced by substances when they are heated inside a flame can be used to identify metals present

- enable you to identify cation and anions present in an unknown sample by performing a series of chemical tests

- show how to perform a titration to obtain quantitative data on the concentration of an acid or alkali.

Practical investigation 22.1: Using flame tests to identify metals

KEY WORDS

anion: a negative ion which would be attracted to the anode in electrolysis

cation: a positive ion which would be attracted to the cathode in electrolysis

titration: a method of quantitative analysis using solutions; one solution is slowly added to a known volume of another solution using a burette until an endpoint is reached

titre: the volume of solution added from the burette during a titration

IN THIS INVESTIGATION YOU WILL:

- learn the colours of the flames produced by lithium, potassium, sodium and copper

- use what you learn to help identify some unknown samples.

YOU WILL NEED:

- Bunsen burner • seven wooden splints (soaked) • heat-resistant mat
- test-tube rack • beaker (250 cm³) • solutions of the following salts: lithium chloride, sodium chloride, copper chloride, potassium chloride, sample X, sample Y and sample Z (all at a concentration between 0.2 and 0.5 mol/dm³) • safety glasses • lab coat
- gloves.

Safety

- Wear eye protection at all times.
- Lithium chloride and copper chloride are harmful.
- Sample Z is an irritant.
- Stand up when using the Bunsen burner to heat the splints.

Getting started

The splints you will use have been soaked in distilled water overnight; however, they may still catch fire when heated. Take a splint and hold it in the flame until it is alight. Practise extinguishing the splint in the beaker of water. If any of your splints catch fire while you are completing a flame test, immediately place the splint into the beaker of water.

Method

1 Half fill the beaker with tap water. You will use this beaker to dispose of your used splints.

2 Place your splint into the solution of lithium chloride and allow the splint to soak for a few minutes.

3 Set up the Bunsen burner and heat-resistant mat.

4 Remove the splint from the solution of lithium chloride and heat the splint in the Bunsen using a blue flame (Figure 22.1). Record the colour observed in the table in the Recording data section.

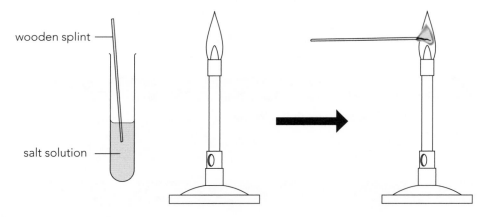

Figure 22.1: Setup for flame tests.

5 Dispose of your splint in the beaker of water.

6 Repeat steps 2–5 with each of the other samples.

Recording data

1   Fill in the table below with your observations from the investigations.

Sample	Colour observed
Lithium chloride	
Sodium chloride	
Copper chloride	
Potassium chloride	
Sample X	
Sample Y	
Sample Z	

Analysis

2   From your results, suggest which metal was contained in samples X, Y and Z.

Sample X ....

Sample Y ....

Sample Z ....

Evaluation

3   Which unknown sample could you not identify?

....

4   Where could you find information to help you identify this sample?

....

5   Suggest a suitable control for this investigation.

....

Practical investigation 22.2: Identifying anions

IN THIS INVESTIGATION YOU WILL:

- learn the test and results for anions

- identify anions using a series of qualitative tests.

YOU WILL NEED:

- test-tube rack • eight test-tubes • pipettes • nitric acid (2.0 mol/dm³)
- Bunsen burner • heat-resistant mat • aluminium foil • red litmus paper • rubber stopper and delivery tube • spatula • calcium carbonate • potassium sulfate
- potassium iodide (0.2 mol/dm³) • sodium bromide • limewater (0.02 mol/dm³)
- barium nitrate solution (0.1 mol/dm³) • silver nitrate solution (0.02 mol/dm³)
- ammonia solution (1.0 mol/dm³) • copper chloride
- potassium sulfite solution (0.2 mol/dm³) • copper(II) nitrate(V) solution (0.01 mol/dm³)
- dilute hydrochloric acid (0.4 mol/dm³) • sodium hydroxide solution (0.4 mol/dm³)
- potassium manganate(VII) solution (0.2 mol/dm³) • safety glasses
- lab coat • gloves.

Safety

- Wear eye protection throughout.

- Nitric acid is corrosive.

- Sodium hydroxide and ammonia solution are irritants.

- Copper chloride and barium nitrate are toxic.

- Potassium manganate(VII) is an irritant, harmful if swallowed and can stain skin.

- Potassium sulfite solution is harmful and corrosive.

- Copper(II) nitrate(V) solution is harmful.

- Take care not to breathe in the fumes produced when heating the copper(II) nitrate(V) solution. Ensure the laboratory is well ventilated.

- Limewater and hydrochloric acid are both moderate hazards.

Getting started

This investigation consists of many different tests. Read the method and plan the order in which you will complete the tests in order to enable you to work efficiently. You will also need to identify which equipment you will need for each test.

Test	Equipment needed

Method

Tests can be completed in any order.

Testing for carbonates

1   Add two spatulas of calcium carbonate to a clean test-tube. Half fill another test-tube with limewater. Take the delivery tube and place the end of the tube so that it is submerged in the limewater.

2   Using a pipette, add approximately $2\,cm^3$ of nitric acid to the calcium carbonate. Immediately close the tube using the rubber stopper (Figure 22.2). Observe the reaction in both tubes and record your results in the table in the Recording data section.

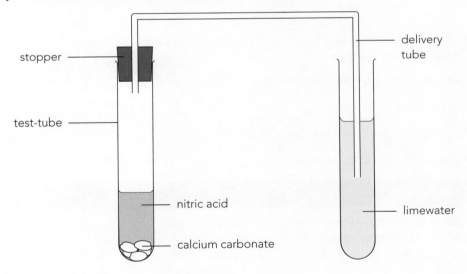

Figure 22.2: Apparatus for testing for carbonates.

Testing for chlorides, bromides and iodides

1   Add two spatulas of copper chloride to a clean test-tube.

2   Half fill the test-tube with nitric acid.

3   Gently shake the tube so that the solid dissolves.

4 Using a pipette, add 2 cm³ of silver nitrate solution to the test-tube. In the results table in the Recording data section, record the colour of the precipitate formed.

5 Using a pipette, slowly add a few drops of ammonia solution. Record whether the precipitate dissolves or not.

6 Repeat steps 1–5 with sodium bromide and then potassium iodide instead of copper chloride.

Testing for sulfates

1 Add two spatulas of potassium sulfate to a clean test-tube.

2 Half fill the test-tube with nitric acid.

3 Gently shake the test-tube so that the solid dissolves.

4 Using a pipette, add 2 cm³ of barium nitrate solution to the test-tube. Record the colour of the precipitate formed in the results table in the Recording data section.

Testing for sulfites

1 Add approximately 2 cm³ of potassium sulfite solution to a clean test-tube.

2 Using a pipette, add 2 cm³ of dilute hydrochloric acid to the test-tube.

3 Add a few drops of aqueous potassium manganate(VII) solution to the test-tube. Record the colour change in the results table in the Recording data section.

Testing for nitrates

1 Hold a damp piece of red litmus paper over the mouth of the test-tube. Record the result in the results table in the Recording data section.

2 Fill a test-tube to about 3 cm depth with copper(II) nitrate(V) solution.

3 Add 2 cm³ of sodium hydroxide solution.

4 Place a small strip of aluminium foil in the test-tube.

5 Using the Bunsen burner, carefully heat the test-tube.

> **TIP**
>
> Hold the damp piece of litmus paper over the mouth of the test-tube for 5–10 seconds to allow the colour change to take place.

Recording data

1   Complete the results table.

Ion being tested	Observations
Carbonate	
Chloride	
Bromide	
Iodide	
Sulfate	
Sulfite	
Nitrate	

Analysis

2   What can you conclude from the results of the carbonate test about the identity of the gas produced?

....

....

3   If sodium chloride was added to nitric acid, followed by silver nitrate solution, what colour precipitate would be formed?

....

....

4   What is the name of the salt formed during the sulfate test?

....

5   Using your knowledge of testing for gases, name the gas produced during the nitrate test.

....

REFLECTION

Think about your organisational skills. What have you learnt about the importance of good organisation when performing investigations?

Do you think you are well organised in your practical work?

What areas could you improve?

....

....

....

Practical investigation 22.3: Identifying cations

IN THIS INVESTIGATION YOU WILL:

- learn the test and results for cations

- identify cations using a series of qualitative tests.

YOU WILL NEED:

- test-tube rack • test-tubes • test-tube holder/clamp • pipettes • Bunsen burner • heat-resistant mat • red litmus paper • tongs • solutions of: sodium hydroxide (0.2 mol/dm³), ammonia solution (2.0 mol/dm³), copper(II) sulfate, iron(II) carbonate, iron(III) sulfate, chromium(III) potassium sulfate, calcium chloride, zinc sulfate, aluminium sulfate (all at 0.1 mol/dm³) • safety glasses • lab coat • gloves.

Safety

- Wear eye protection throughout.

- Aluminium sulfate is corrosive and a moderate hazard.

- Iron(III) sulfate is an irritant and a moderate hazard.

- Chromium(III) potassium sulfate is an irritant and a moderate hazard.

- Zinc sulfate is an irritant, is corrosive, a moderate hazard and hazardous to the aquatic environment. Waste from experiments using zinc sulfate must not be poured down the drain.

- Ammonia solution is corrosive.

- Sodium hydroxide is an irritant.

- Copper(II) sulfate solution is a moderate hazard and hazardous to the aquatic environment. Waste from experiments using copper(II) sulfate must not be poured down the drain.

- Take care not to breathe in the fumes produced when heating the ammonia solution. Ensure the laboratory is well ventilated.

Getting started

In this investigation you will need to use damp litmus paper to identify a gas. Holding litmus paper in tongs can be very difficult; you should practise firmly holding the litmus paper using the tongs before starting the practical.

Method

Test for ammonium ions

1   Add 2 cm³ of ammonium ion solution and 2 cm³ of sodium hydroxide to a test-tube. Set up the Bunsen burner on the heat-resistant mat. Heat the solution gently. Using the tongs, hold a piece of damp red litmus paper over the mouth of the tube (Figure 22.3). Record your observations in the results table in the Recording data section.

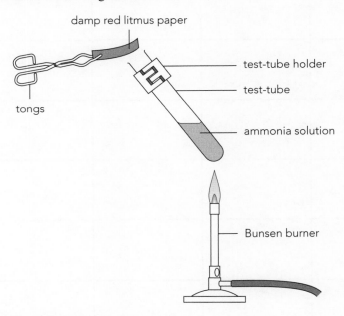

Figure 22.3: Apparatus to test for ammonia gas.

Test for metal cations

1   Add 2 cm³ of copper(II) sulfate to a test-tube in a test-tube rack. Slowly (drop by drop) add 2 cm³ of sodium hydroxide. Record your observations in the results table in the Recording data section.

2   Add 2 cm³ more sodium hydroxide solution. Record your observations in the results table.

3   Add 2 cm³ of copper(II) sulfate to a clean test-tube. Slowly add 2 cm³ of ammonia solution. Record your observations in the results table.

4   Add 2 cm³ more ammonia solution. Record your observations in the results table.

5   Repeat steps 1–4 with each of the different cation solutions.

Recording data

1   Complete the results table.

Cation solution	Result when sodium hydroxide is added	Result when excess sodium hydroxide is added	Result when ammonia solution is added	Result when excess ammonia solution is added
Ammonia solution				
Copper(II) sulfate				
Iron(II) carbonate				
Iron(III) sulfate				
Chromium(III) potassium sulfate				
Calcium chloride				
Zinc sulfate				
Aluminium sulfate				

Handling data

2   In the space provided, design a flow diagram that you could use to identify any of the metal ions in salts. The first question should be 'Is a precipitate formed when sodium hydroxide is added?'

TIP
A flow diagram is a useful way to display a series of steps in a process. Each step is linked by an arrow.

Analysis

3 Look at your result for the damp red litmus paper test you did on the heated ammonia solution after you added sodium hydroxide. What does this result tell you about the identity of the gas produced?

....

....

4 A sample containing a cation is being tested. Use the results below to identify the cation present:

Result when sodium hydroxide added = white precipitate formed

Result when excess sodium hydroxide added = precipitate dissolves giving a clear solution

Result when ammonia solution added = white precipitate formed

Result when excess ammonia solution added = precipitate dissolves

The cations in the investigation are:

....

Evaluation

5 Why is it important that clean test-tubes are used for each experiment?

....

Practical investigation 22.4: Acid–base titration

IN THIS INVESTIGATION YOU WILL:

- determine the volume of acid needed to neutralise a known volume of alkali using the titration-method

- calculate the concentration of the acid used, by taking careful readings of measurements

- use an indicator with a specific endpoint (a point where a clear observable change takes place).

YOU WILL NEED:

- burette (50 cm^3) • pipette or measuring cylinder (25 cm^3)
- clamp stand and burette clamp • white tile • funnel
- conical flask (100 cm^3 or 250 cm^3) • methyl orange indicator
- sodium hydroxide solution (1.0 mol/dm^3) • dilute hydrochloric acid (1.0 mol/dm^3)
- safety glasses • lab coat • gloves.

Safety

- Wear eye protection throughout.

- Sodium hydroxide is corrosive and harmful.

- Methyl orange indicator is corrosive, flammable, a health and moderate hazard, hazardous to the aquatic environment, and is acutely toxic.

- Hydrochloric acid is a moderate hazard.

Getting started

Practise neutralising a small volume of sodium hydroxide with hydrochloric acid so that you are familiar with the colour change that occurs. Add 3 cm^3 of sodium hydroxide to a conical flask. Add one or two drops of methyl orange indicator to the conical flask. Using a pipette, add hydrochloric acid one drop at a time until you see a colour change.

TIP

Methyl orange is often used for titrations because it shows a distinct colour change from yellow in basic conditions to red in acidic conditions.

Method

1   Measure 25 cm³ of sodium hydroxide using the measuring cylinder and pour the liquid into the conical flask.

2   Add five drops of methyl orange.

3   Rinse the burette with distilled water and then with hydrochloric acid. Make sure that the burette below the tap is also filled. You may need to shake the burette gently while the tap is open to remove any air bubbles. Close the burette tap and fill the burette with hydrochloric acid to a whole number near zero. (It can be zero but does not need to be. You should record the exact value.)

4   Secure the burette in the clamp stand and place the conical flask on a white tile underneath it (Figure 22.4).

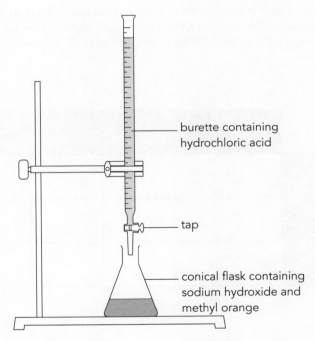

burette containing hydrochloric acid

tap

conical flask containing sodium hydroxide and methyl orange

Figure 22.4: Apparatus to perform a titration.

5   Slowly add the acid to the alkali a few cm³ at a time until there is a permanent colour change.

TIP

Swirl the liquid inside the conical flask after you add each portion of acid using a twisting, circular movement of the flask.

6 Record the final volume in the burette.

7 Calculate the volume (titre) that was added to cause the change. This is your rough value.

8 Pour away the contents of the conical flask and rinse it out with water. Repeat steps 1–4.

9 This time you have a rough value at which the colour change will occur so you can add the acid steadily a few cm^3 at a time until you reach a few cm^3 less than you did for your rough value and then slowly add the acid to get a more accurate value. Repeat the titration three times and then calculate the mean.

See the Practical skills and support section at the start of this workbook for more information on how to read a burette.

> **TIP**
>
> The first run in a titration experiment to obtain a rough value for the titre is known as a trial or pilot run.

Recording data

Think carefully about how you will record your results for this titration. How many decimal places will you record your data to? The more decimal places, the more precise your data will be. Look at your burette carefully. What is the smallest scale division? This will be different for various types of burette but it should be at least to $0.1\,cm^3$.

1 Complete the results table.

	Rough value from pilot run	1	2	3
Final reading / cm^3				
Initial reading / cm^3				
Volume of acid used (titre) / cm^3				

Handling data

You can now use the mean volume used to calculate the concentration of the hydrochloric acid. In this section give all of your answers to three decimal places.

2 Calculate the molar concentration of the sodium hydroxide in the conical flask.

....

....

3 How many moles of hydrochloric acid would be needed to neutralise the number of moles of sodium hydroxide for part **2**?

....

....

4 Calculate the mean volume of hydrochloric acid needed to neutralise the sodium hydroxide.

....

....

> **TIP**
>
> Remember to ignore your rough results from the pilot run and any anomalous results.

Analysis

5 What was the concentration of hydrochloric acid used?

> **TIP**
>
> You will need to convert your results from cm^3 to dm^3. 1 cm^3 is equal to 0.001 dm^3.

....

....

Evaluation

6 Why did you ignore the rough results when calculating your mean?

....

....

7 What does 'anomalous' mean?

....

8 Why was it necessary to swirl the conical flask after adding each portion of acid?

....

....

9 Why did you use a white tile?

....

....

10 Were there any problems with your investigation that meant your data might have been unreliable?

....

....

11 Can you suggest a way to improve your investigation so that your results were more reliable?

....

....

REFLECTION

Titration is a very important experimental technique in quantitative chemistry.

Do you understand why all of the different steps are performed in a titration?

Did you find it easy or difficult to perform the practical tasks?

EXAM-STYLE QUESTIONS

1 A student is investigating the colours produced by different solutions using a flame test.

    a **Suggest** a safety precaution she should take while performing the flame tests.

    .... **[1]**

The student had three unknown compounds: A, B and C.

Sample	Flame colour	Metal
A	lilac	
B	green	
C	red	

    b Add the names of the metals present in each sample to the table. **[3]**

                                                                       [Total: 4]

COMMAND WORD

suggest: apply knowledge and understanding to situations where there are a range of valid responses in order to make proposals/ put forward considerations

CONTINUED

2 A student is trying to identify an unknown salt. She first makes a visual observation of the salt. It is a white powder. She then adds dilute hydrochloric acid to the powder.

  a **State** what the student would expect to see if the powder contained a carbonate.

  .... [1]

COMMAND WORD

state: express in clear terms

From the results of the first test, the student knows that the substance is not a carbonate. She adds some dilute nitric acid to a sample of the powder and then some silver nitrate solution. A pale white or creamy precipitate is formed.

  b Suggest which two anions the sample might contain.

  .... [2]

  c Suggest what further test the student could do to identify which of the two anions identified in part **b** are in the sample.

  .... [2]

The student now wants to identify the cation present. She adds a small amount of sodium hydroxide and then warms the test-tube.

  d State the test for the presence of ammonia gas being given off.

  .... [1]

  e **Describe** the result of the test you stated in part d if ammonia gas were being given off.

  .... [1]

COMMAND WORD

describe: state the points of a topic / give characteristics and main features

No ammonia gas was given off but a white precipitate was formed. Precipitate dissolves with excess sodium hydroxide.

Ammonia solution was added to a fresh sample of the powder. A white precipitate was formed that was soluble in excess ammonia solution.

  f State the cation present in the sample.

  .... [1]

  [Total: 8]

CONTINUED

3 Look at the results table below and write the results of each test you would expect for the salts listed.

Salt	Sodium hydroxide added / and in excess	Ammonia solution added / and in excess	Dilute nitric acid added and silver nitrate added
Calcium chloride			
Zinc iodide			
Chromium(III) bromide			

[9]

4 You have been given a bottle with a solution containing a salt with a magnesium cation but an unknown anion. Plan an investigation to explain how you would identify the anion present in the solution.

....

....

....

....

....

....

....

....

....

....

....

....

....

....

[12]

> Glossary

Command Words

Below are the Cambridge International definitions for command words that may be used in exams. The information in this section is taken from the Cambridge International syllabus (0620/0971) for examination from 2023. You should always refer to the appropriate syllabus document for the year of your examination to confirm the details and for more information. The syllabus document is available on the Cambridge International website www.cambridgeinternational.org.

analyse: examine in detail to show meaning, identify elements and the relationship between them

calculate: work out from given facts, figures or information

compare: identify/comment on similarities and/or differences

consider: review and respond to given information

contrast: identify/comment on differences

deduce: conclude from available information

define: give precise meaning

demonstrate: show how or give an example

describe: state the points of a topic / give characteristics and main features

determine: establish an answer using the information available

discuss: write about issue(s) or topic(s) in depth in a structured way

evaluate: judge or calculate the quality, importance, amount, or value of something

examine: investigate closely, in detail

explain: set out purposes or reasons / make the relationships between things evident / provide why and/ or how and support with relevant evidence

give: produce an answer from a given source or recall/memory

identify: name/select/recognise

justify: support a case with evidence/argument

predict: suggest what may happen based on available information

show (that): provide structured evidence that leads to a given result

sketch: make a simple freehand drawing showing the key features, taking care over proportions

state: express in clear terms

suggest: apply knowledge and understanding to situations where there are a range of valid responses in order to make proposals / put forward considerations

Key Words

acid: a substance that dissolves in water, producing $H^+(aq)$ ions – a solution of an acid turns litmus red and has a pH below 7. Acids act as proton donors

acid rain: rain that has been made more acidic than normal by the presence of dissolved pollutants such as sulfur dioxide (SO_2) and oxides of nitrogen (nitrogen oxides, NO_x)

alkalis: soluble bases that produce $OH^-(aq)$ ions in water – a solution of an alkali turns litmus blue and has a pH above 7

alloy: mixtures of elements (usually metals) designed to have the properties useful for a particular purpose, e.g. solder (an alloy of tin and lead) has a low melting point

anion: a negative ion which would be attracted to the anode in electrolysis

anode: the electrode in any type of cell at which oxidation (the loss of electrons) takes place – in electrolysis it is the positive electrode

antacids: compounds used medically to treat indigestion by neutralising excess stomach acid

aqueous bromine: bromine dissolved in water

atomic number (or proton number) (Z): the number of protons in the nucleus of an atom

base: a substance that neutralises an acid, producing a salt and water as the only products. Bases act as proton acceptors

biofuel: fuels made directly from the products of living matter, e.g. ethanol

blast furnace: a furnace for extracting metals (particularly iron) by reduction with carbon that uses hot air blasted in at the base of the furnace to raise the temperature

boiling point: the temperature at which a liquid boils, when the pressure of the gas created above the liquid equals atmospheric pressure

catalyst: a substance that increases the rate of a chemical reaction but itself remains unchanged at the end of the reaction

catalytic cracking: the decomposition of long-chain alkanes into alkenes and alkanes of lower relative molecular mass; involves passing the larger alkane molecules over a catalyst heated to 500 °C

cathode: the electrode in any type of cell at which reduction (the gain of electrons) takes place; in electrolysis it is the negative electrode

cation: a positive ion which would be attracted to the cathode in electrolysis

chemical formula: a shorthand method of representing chemical elements and compounds using the symbols of the elements

chemical symbol: a letter or group of letters representing an element in a chemical formula

chromatography: a technique employed for the separation of mixtures of dissolved substances, which was originally used to separate coloured dyes

combustion: a chemical reaction in which a substance reacts with oxygen – the reaction is exothermic

compound: a substance formed by the chemical combination of two or more elements in fixed proportions

corrosion: the process that takes place when metals and alloys are chemically attacked by oxygen, water or any other substances found in their immediate environment

covalent bonding: chemical bonding formed by the sharing of one or more pairs of electrons between two atoms

displacement reaction: a reaction in which a more reactive element displaces a less reactive element from a solution of its salt

distillation: the process of boiling a liquid and then condensing the vapour produced, back into a liquid: used to purify liquids and to separate liquids from solutions

dynamic (chemical) equilibrium: two chemical reactions, one the reverse of the other, taking place at the same time, where the concentrations of the reactants and products remain constant because the rate at which the forward reaction occurs is the same as that of the reverse reaction

electrical conductor: a substance that conducts electricity but is not chemically changed in the process

electrolysis: the breakdown of an ionic compound, molten or in aqueous solution, by the use of electricity

electrolyte: an ionic compound that will conduct electricity when it is molten or dissolved in water; electrolytes will not conduct electricity when solid

electron: a subatomic particle with negligible mass and a charge of –1; electrons are present in all atoms, located in the shells (energy levels) outside the nucleus

electron shells (energy levels): (of electrons) the allowed energies of electrons in atoms – electrons fill these shells (or levels) starting with the one closest to the nucleus

electroplating: a process of electrolysis in which a metal object is coated (plated) with a layer of another metal

element: a substance that cannot be further divided into simpler substances by chemical methods; all the atoms of an element contain the same number of protons

empirical formula: a formula for a compound that shows the simplest ratio of atoms present

endothermic changes: a process or chemical reaction that takes in heat from the surroundings. ΔH for an endothermic change has a positive value.

evaporation: a process occurring at the surface of a liquid, involving the change of state from a liquid into a vapour at a temperature below the boiling point

exothermic changes: a process or chemical reaction in which heat energy is produced and released to the surroundings. ΔH for an exothermic change has a negative value.

fermentation: a reaction carried out using a living organism, usually a yeast or bacteria, to produce a useful chemical compound; most usually refers to the production of ethanol

fertiliser: a substance added to the soil to replace essential elements lost when crops are harvested, which enables crops to grow faster and increases the yield

filtration: the separation of a solid from a liquid, using a fine filter paper that does not allow the solid to pass through

fossil fuels: fuels, such as coal, oil and natural gas, formed underground over geological periods of time from the remains of plants and animals

freezing point: the temperature at which a liquid turns into a solid – it has the same value as the melting point; a pure substance has a sharp freezing point

fuel: a substance that can be used as a source of energy, usually by burning (combustion)

galvanising: the protection of iron and steel objects by coating with a layer of zinc

greenhouse effect: the natural phenomenon in which thermal energy from the Sun is 'trapped' at the Earth's surface by certain gases in the atmosphere (greenhouse gases)

greenhouse gas: a gas that absorbs heat reflected from the surface of the Earth, stopping it escaping the atmosphere

groups: vertical columns of the Periodic Table containing elements with similar chemical properties; atoms of elements in the same group have the same number of electrons in their outer energy levels

homologous series: a family of similar compounds with similar chemical properties due to the presence of the same functional group

hydrated salts: salts whose crystals contain combined water (*water of crystallisation*) as part of the structure

hydrocarbons: organic compounds which contain carbon and hydrogen only; the alkanes and alkenes are two series of hydrocarbons

indicator: a substance that changes colour when added to acidic or alkaline solutions, e.g. litmus or thymolphthalein

insoluble: a substance that does not dissolve in a particular solvent

intermolecular forces: the weak attractive forces which act between molecules

ionic bonding: a strong electrostatic force of attraction between oppositely charged ions

ions: charged particles made from an atom, or groups of atoms (compound ions), by the loss or gain of electrons

isotopes: atoms of the same element that have the same proton number but a different nucleon number; they have different numbers of neutrons in their nuclei; some isotopes are radioactive because their nuclei are unstable (radioisotopes)

lime: a white solid known chemically as calcium oxide (CaO), produced by heating limestone; it can be used to counteract soil acidity, to manufacture calcium hydroxide (slaked lime) and also as a drying agent

limestone: a form of calcium carbonate ($CaCO_3$)

malleable: a word used to describe the property that metals can be bent and beaten into sheets

mass number (or nucleon number) (A): the total number of protons and neutrons in the nucleus of an atom

matter: anything that occupies space and has mass

melting point (m.p): the temperature at which a solid turns into a liquid – it has the same value as the freezing point; a pure substance has a sharp melting point

metals: a class of chemical elements (and alloys) that have a characteristic shiny appearance and are good conductors of heat and electricity

methyl orange: an acid–base indicator that is red in acidic and yellow in alkaline solutions

mole: the measure of amount of substance in chemistry; 1 mole of a substance has a mass equal to its relative formula mass in grams – that amount of substance contains 6.02×10^{23} (the Avogadro constant) atoms, molecules or formula units depending on the substance considered

neutralisation: a chemical reaction between an acid and a base to produce a salt and water only; summarised by the ionic equation $H^+(aq) + OH^-(aq) \rightarrow H_2O(l)$

neutron: an uncharged subatomic particle present in the nuclei of atoms – a neutron has a mass of 1 relative to a proton

ore: a naturally occurring mineral from which a metal can be extracted

oxidation: there are three definitions of oxidation:
i a reaction in which oxygen is added to an element or compound
ii a reaction involving the loss of electrons from an atom, molecule or ion
iii a reaction in which the oxidation state of an element is increased

percentage yield: a measure of the actual yield of a reaction when carried out experimentally compared to the theoretical yield calculated from the equation:

$$\text{percentage yield} = \frac{\text{actual yield}}{\text{predicted yield}} \times 100$$

period: a horizontal row of the Periodic Table

Periodic Table: a table of elements arranged in order of increasing proton number (atomic number) to show the similarities of the chemical elements with related electronic configurations

pH scale: a scale running from below 0 to 14, used for expressing the acidity or alkalinity of a solution; a neutral solution has a pH of 7

photosynthesis: the chemical process by which plants synthesise glucose from atmospheric carbon dioxide and water giving off oxygen as a by-product: the energy required for the process is captured from sunlight by chlorophyll molecules in the green leaves of the plants

plastics: polymers that can be moulded or shaped by the action of heat and pressure

polymer: a substance consisting of very large molecules made by polymerising a large number of repeating units or monomers

precipitation: the sudden formation of a solid when either two solutions are mixed or a gas is bubbled into a solution

precipitation reaction: a reaction in which an insoluble salt is prepared from solutions of two suitable soluble salts

proton: a subatomic particle with a relative mass of 1 and a charge +1 found in the nucleus of all atoms

proton number (or atomic number) (Z): the number of protons in the nucleus of an atom (see also **atomic number**)

reaction rate: a measure of how fast a reaction takes place

reactivity series of metals: an order of reactivity, giving the most reactive metal first, based on results from a range of experiments involving metals reacting with oxygen, water, dilute hydrochloric acid and metal salt solutions

redox reaction: a reaction involving both reduction and oxidation

reduction: there are three definitions of reduction:
i a reaction in which oxygen is removed from a compound
ii a reaction involving the gain of electrons by an atom, molecule or ion
iii a reaction in which the oxidation state of an element is decreased

relative atomic mass (A_r): the average mass of naturally occurring atoms of an element on a scale where the carbon-12 atom has a mass of exactly 12 units

relative formula mass (M_r): the sum of all the relative atomic masses of the atoms present in a 'formula unit' of a substance (see also **relative molecular mass**)

relative molecular mass (M_r): the sum of all the relative atomic masses of the atoms present in a molecule (see also **relative formula mass**)

respiration: the chemical reaction (a combustion reaction) by which biological cells release the energy stored in glucose for use by the cell or the body; the reaction is exothermic and produces carbon dioxide and water as the chemical by-products

reversible reaction: a chemical reaction that can go either forwards or backwards, depending on the conditions

rust: a loose, orange–brown, flaky layer of hydrated iron(III) oxide, $Fe_2O_3 \cdot xH_2O$, found on the surface of iron or steel

sacrificial protection: a method of rust protection involving the attachment of blocks of a metal more reactive than iron to a structure; this metal is corroded rather than the iron or steel structure

salts: ionic compounds made by the neutralisation of an acid with a base (or alkali), e.g. copper(II) sulfate and potassium nitrate

saturated: an organic compound containing the maximum number of hydrogen atoms whilst also containing no double or triple bonds, e.g. alkanes

soluble: a solute that dissolves in a particular solvent

solute: the solid substance that has dissolved in a liquid (the solvent) to form a solution

solvent: the liquid that dissolves the solid solute to form a solution; water is the most common solvent but liquids in organic chemistry that can act as solvents are called *organic solvents*

state symbols: symbols used to show the physical state of the reactants and products in a chemical reaction: they are s (solid), l (liquid), g (gas) and aq (in solution in water)

subatomic particles: very small particles – protons, neutrons and electrons – from which all atoms are made

thermal conductor: a substance that efficiently transfers heat energy by conduction

thermal decomposition: the breakdown of a compound due to heating

titration: a method of quantitative analysis using solutions; one solution is slowly added to a known volume of another solution using a burette until an endpoint is reached

titre: the volume of solution added from the burette during a titration

universal indicator: a mixture of indicators that has different colours in solutions of different pH

unsaturated: an organic compound that contains double or triple bonds between the carbon atoms, e.g. alkenes

variable: any factor in an *experiment* that can be changed (independent variable), measured (dependent variable) or controlled (controlled variable)

word equation: a summary of a chemical reaction using the chemical names of the reactants and products

The Periodic Table of Elements

Key

atomic number
atomic symbol
name
relative atomic mass

I	II		III	IV	V	VI	VII	VIII
		1 H hydrogen 1						2 He helium 4
3 Li lithium 7	4 Be beryllium 9		5 B boron 11	6 C carbon 12	7 N nitrogen 14	8 O oxygen 16	9 F fluorine 19	10 Ne neon 20
11 Na sodium 23	12 Mg magnesium 24		13 Al aluminium 27	14 Si silicon 28	15 P phosphorus 31	16 S sulfur 32	17 Cl chlorine 35.5	18 Ar argon 40
19 K potassium 39	20 Ca calcium 40	21 Sc scandium 45 / 22 Ti titanium 48 / 23 V vanadium 51 / 24 Cr chromium 52 / 25 Mn manganese 55 / 26 Fe iron 56 / 27 Co cobalt 59 / 28 Ni nickel 59 / 29 Cu copper 64 / 30 Zn zinc 65	31 Ga gallium 70	32 Ge germanium 73	33 As arsenic 75	34 Se selenium 79	35 Br bromine 80	36 Kr krypton 84
37 Rb rubidium 85	38 Sr strontium 88	39 Y yttrium 89 / 40 Zr zirconium 91 / 41 Nb niobium 93 / 42 Mo molybdenum 96 / 43 Tc technetium - / 44 Ru ruthenium 101 / 45 Rh rhodium 103 / 46 Pd palladium 106 / 47 Ag silver 108 / 48 Cd cadmium 112	49 In indium 115	50 Sn tin 119	51 Sb antimony 122	52 Te tellurium 128	53 I iodine 127	54 Xe xenon 131
55 Cs caesium 133	56 Ba barium 137	57–71 lanthanoids / 72 Hf hafnium 178 / 73 Ta tantalum 181 / 74 W tungsten 184 / 75 Re rhenium 186 / 76 Os osmium 190 / 77 Ir iridium 192 / 78 Pt platinum 195 / 79 Au gold 197 / 80 Hg mercury 201	81 Tl thallium 204	82 Pb lead 207	83 Bi bismuth 209	84 Po polonium -	85 At astatine -	86 Rn radon -
87 Fr francium -	88 Ra radium -	89–103 actinoids / 104 Rf rutherfordium - / 105 Db dubnium - / 106 Sg seaborgium - / 107 Bh bohrium - / 108 Hs hassium - / 109 Mt meitnerium - / 110 Ds darmstadtium - / 111 Rg roentgenium - / 112 Cn copernicium -	113 Nh nihonium -	114 Fl flerovium -	115 Mc moscovium -	116 Lv livermorium -	117 Ts tennessine -	118 Og oganesson -

lanthanoids

| 57 La lanthanum 139 | 58 Ce cerium 140 | 59 Pr praseodymium 141 | 60 Nd neodymium 144 | 61 Pm promethium - | 62 Sm samarium 150 | 63 Eu europium 152 | 64 Gd gadolinium 157 | 65 Tb terbium 159 | 66 Dy dysprosium 163 | 67 Ho holmium 165 | 68 Er erbium 167 | 69 Tm thulium 169 | 70 Yb ytterbium 173 | 71 Lu lutetium 175 |

actinoids

| 89 Ac actinium - | 90 Th thorium 232 | 91 Pa protactinium 231 | 92 U uranium 238 | 93 Np neptunium - | 94 Pu plutonium - | 95 Am americium - | 96 Cm curium - | 97 Bk berkelium - | 98 Cf californium - | 99 Es einsteinium - | 100 Fm fermium - | 101 Md mendelevium - | 102 No nobelium - | 103 Lr lawrencium - |

The volume of one mole of any gas is 24 dm^3 at room temperature and pressure (r.t.p.).